1 *plus one* = TEN

The Secret LEADERSHIP Formula only ELITE Leaders Know

Former 10-year HARLEM GLOBETROTTER leader, KEVIN DALEY, decodes the secret leadership formula you must know to become an elite leader

Copyright © 2018 by Kevin Daley
All rights reserved. This book or any portion thereof may not be reproduced or used in any manner whatsoever without the express written permission of the publisher except for the use of brief quotations in a book review.

Printed in the United States of America

First Printing, 2018

ISBN 978-0-9906449-1-0

3DQUEST

Grand Prairie, TX

Ordering Information:

Quantity sales. Special discounts are available on quantity purchases by corporations, associations, and others. For details, send email to info@kevindaleyspeaks.com.

www.KevinDaleySpeaks.com

Social Media: @mrtrotter21

To my lovely wife Danielle – thank you for accepting me with all my flaws and for always supporting me as I pursue my dreams. I loved you yesterday, I love you today, and I will love you tomorrow.

1 *plus one* = TEN

*The Secret LEADERSHIP Formula
only ELITE Leaders Know*

CONTENTS

Warm-Up: *Start Smiling!* 1

Chapter One: *Synergize* 12

Chapter Two: *Motivate* 28

Chapter Three: *Impact* 38

Chapter Four: *Lead* 46

Chapter Five: *Empower* 54

Chapter Six: *Smile* 67

Cool Down: *Keep Smiling!* 79

Warm-Up:
Start Smiling!

"You don't need a title to be a leader." - Mark Sanborn

I have been in the business of handing out smiles through a well-known, yet odd mixture of ingredients. My smile ingredients consisted of one basketball, countless crazy pranks, daily powerful athleticism, one fabulous team and numerous jaw-dropping feats of basketball skill. And when combined, these ingredients resulted in the greatest athletic show in the history of organized sports: the Harlem Globetrotters. The team, founded in 1926 in Chicago, Illinois, started out as an exhibition basketball team. By the 1940s, the Globetrotters began to use comedy and gags as part of their basketball demonstrations, and ever since, the Harlem Globetrotters have been known for three things: amazing basketball, hilarious antics and putting smiles on people's faces.

Now, you're probably thinking, *that's definitely* not *the business I'm in!* You might be a manager or an executive in a setting that deals in technology development, advertising or manufacturing, and handing out smiles is simply not your priority. Well, I hope to convince you otherwise, because the smiles I'm talking about handing out are not to your *customers*, but to your team, which creates your product or service *for* the customers.

And in fact, those smiles could be the difference between working for a decent company or a great one. It could be the difference between a reasonably satisfied customer base and a *loyal lead-generating* customer base, which relays your outstanding reputation to their spheres of influence.

Two Ways to Hand Out Smiles: Artificially and Naturally

Any company executive can decide to try and create an artificial spike in team morale. You can take your team to a baseball game (of course basketball would be my choice), have a terrific Christmas party and hand out some bonuses, or use lots of cliché words of encouragement like "great job," "way to go," "good team effort," and it might look like you've created a winner. None of these gestures are inherently bad or ineffective, but if an attempt to increase team morale consists of something you could literally think of the night before and carry out the next day, it is more than likely just a band-aid fix. It may not address a deeper need to create a company-culture smile, which is rooted in a top-to-bottom approach to working as a team. In fact, artificial quick-fix morale-boosters can even stimulate resentment in some team members, with thoughts such as, "I'd rather the GM listen to my ideas than have my manager take me to a stupid hockey game." All of the instant injections you might think of to boost the spirits of your team are best saved as the icing on the cake to a more natural and organic way of thinking about team interaction and productivity.

In contrast to attempting to create shot-in-the-dark happiness events, what I am going to show you in this book is a more natural way to hand out smiles. In essence, the smiles you are aiming for consist of heart-felt company loyalty (a rare commodity in this era), high-initiative teamwork motivated by genuine affection and respect for the team and its leader(s), and the irreplaceable sense of satisfaction that what the team is achieving *matters*. Let me show you what I mean as I unpack each of these company-culture smile creators.

Heart-Felt Company Loyalty

Decades ago an employee was proud to be called "a company man," meaning he was loyal to a fault to the company name and reputation. Back then the idea of starting and ending your career with the same company was normal, not peculiar. That is no longer the case, and the impact is devastating for companies that cannot keep up with employee dissatisfaction. Employees who are not "all in" cost organizations about *a half-trillion* dollars annually. And even among employees who report being completely committed to their current situation, 37% of them are still looking for new opportunities.[i] This makes achieving development traction from a consistent team roster all the more difficult.

The good news—and the reason for this book—is that studies show organizations with high employee engagement outperform those with low employee engagement by 202%.[ii] Meaning, if you can build truly lasting joy in your team, which is the outcome of high-satisfaction team achievements, then the toehold you gain moving forward makes your team not just a collection of individual experts in their field, but an expert cohesive team working *together*—a unit.

Teamwork Motivated by Affection and Respect for Leadership

One of the great benefits of organized team sports is the experience of the player-coach relationship. Any athlete who has played at a reasonably high level, as I have, can recount stories—stories with emotion and great passion—of a particular coach who highly influenced them. Usually those anecdotes go far beyond the sport itself, and the coach didn't just make the player a better player, he made the player a better *person*. These are the types of leaders a team will follow to the ends of the earth.

For me that person was Wayne Merino, basketball coach at Artesia High School in Lakewood, California. I had transferred in from another school and honestly thought I was pretty good—until I ran up against Coach Merino's high standards, higher expectations and highest integrity. He ran a basketball practice like I had never experienced before and, as a result, I barely made the team, and was thankful just to have a spot. But Coach Merino saw something in me I hadn't yet seen in myself, and he drove me, pushed me, and expected more and more out of me. By the end of the first season, I went from a long-shot walk-on to the captain of the team. Coach Merino not only expected me to play at a high level, he expected me to *lead* at a high level. He became like a second father to me, giving me lessons in leadership and excellence that continue to impact me every day. Today I am still privileged to call him not only "Coach," but my good friend, as well.

Both as a basketball player and as a consultant in the business community, I have often asked myself a simple question about a leader, whether it be a coach or a company executive: *"If I asked the followers (the players or employees) whether that leader genuinely cares about them or not, what is the honest answer I would get?"* I believe the answer to that question can almost instantly diagnose the health of any team. Why? Because team members who believe the team leader honestly cares for them as people—husbands, wives, fathers, mothers—finds that they come to work for more than just a paycheck; they come to *give back to their leader the care they sense from him or her.* It is an observable fact: teams who love their leaders achieve more.

Leaders who think they can achieve team greatness without engendering the affection and respect of their team players are fooling themselves. Affection causes loyalty, which causes productivity and initiative—a heart-felt desire to do great things as a team, both for the leader and for one another.

What We Do Matters

The third company-culture creator consists of the tangible sense that what we do matters. In not-for-profit organizations, this culture is sometimes more easily established since the clients being served demonstrate an easily observable benefit. For example, a foster care agency need only look at the roster of children for whom they provide care to see clearly that they are doing something that matters.

But what if your team is responsible for researching a new technological development for a video game to be released in a year? What is the "why does this matter" answer in that scenario? Certainly, those who are "techie" by natural instinct and aptitude love the nitty-gritty details of that world, but what about the human satisfaction factor? Can you, as the team leader, convince your team that the game they develop will be played by families who are always looking for activities to do together? That this game will make Christmas shopping a little more exciting and bring dads... and sons... and moms... and daughters together? Can they picture the nights of several bags of popcorn, laughter, and a gathering in the family room to play this game?

Bringing the Magic: 1 + 1 = 10

Every accomplishment in human history began with a dream. The capacity to see something that does not exist and then make it reality is fundamental to our very nature as human beings. And every business start-up began with a dream. Most fail; a few succeed. If someone has low-input dreams, they will get low-output results. In other words, if my biggest dream is to deliver pizzas two nights per week to make a little extra cash (certainly nothing wrong with that), then the output will be equal to my input. If I work 10 hours, then I will get 10 hours of income as a result. But what if my dream is to work 10 hours and get *1,000 hours* output as a result—that everything I do has a multiplied result? *This* is the dream that you as a leader already possess!

If you are reading this book, that means you *don't* want to settle for your output simply being equal to input. You *don't* want to be content to have 1 + 1 = 2. Those who dream big understand that there are only 168 hours in every week and therefore, they cannot be responsible for making every facet of their dream come true. Big dreamers like you need to hammer one nail and see a house built. You need to see a dollar invested and $100 returned. You need to see one jumpstart turn into 1,000 engines running. Instead of 1 + 1 = 2, you want to make 1 + 1 = 10.

Breaking Down the Formula

This formula in which your leadership *output* far exceeds your *input* can be understood in three parts; however, we need to take them out of order. First, let's talk about the result, the "10." This is fairly simple: *the "10" consists of the biggest possible result of a vision you have cast*, a result that is surprising even to you.

Some people are naturally born with this ability to see multiplied results before they happen; others need a little more encouragement. Warren Buffett, arguably the greatest individual investor of all time, used money he earned from his paper route to buy some farmland—at the age of 11! He took money he earned the hard way (1 + 1 = 2) and had a vision to use it to buy into something that would improve the output of his work. He used money earned from delivering papers to get involved in a pinball machine business, which was earning him good money by the time he was 15 years old. And, of course, eventually he came to be worth tens of billions of dollars.

Now, before you get overwhelmed with inadequacy, we all acknowledge that Warren Buffett is somewhat of a freak of nature who had something most of us did *not* have: a father and mentor who taught him to think big. He just happened to get a head start from his father's external influence. So, the "10" part of the equation—the outcome of your vision—is a fairly simple concept.

Second, let's talk about the first "1" of the equation. This is quite simply *you*. *You* must look in the mirror and decide which equation you want. I'm not talking about personal wealth or even climbing the ladder of success. I *am* talking about what kind of effectiveness you want to bring to *whatever* you do. Do you want to live a life of 1 + 1 = 2? There is nothing wrong with that, and this is an honorable way to live. But my guess is that you're simply not wired that way. You *do* want to make 1 + 1 = 10; you *do* want to see that your efforts mean something and cause chain reactions of good things to happen.

Even though this is only the introduction to *1 plus one = TEN*, here is the simple, time-tested secret to producing a "10" result rather than a "2" result: *You must set aside part of your time to dream and plan beyond the immediate present.* I'm not talking about planning out your calendar year or even the coming months; I'm talking about taking time to plan life-changing and direction-altering courses of action that will produce results *you no longer must personally make happen.* This is a simple question: Are *you* ready to be the first part of the equation, the first "1," in order to achieve "10?"

Finally, let's talk about the second "1" of the equation. This is the truly magical part of the formula. The other two pieces are easy to understand. But the second "1" is what makes the difference between greatness and mediocrity. This is the secret ingredient, which makes the first "1" (you) into a powerhouse achiever who brings consistent "10" results. This is the intangible quality that all great leaders possess. This is what some have called "the **_IT_** factor"—that a leader simply has "**_IT_**." Well, it's my aim in this book to break down this *intangible* into *tangible* ways of thinking and action items. I believe some people are born with "IT"—with 1 + 1 = 10. But I *also* believe "IT" can be taught and learned. So, what is the second "1," the "IT" that will give you infinitely more *output* than *input*? Welcome to my S.M.I.L.E.S. formula—where 1 + 1 (S.M.I.L.E.S.) = 10. Let the magic begin!

1 + 1 (S.M.I.L.E.S.) = 10

I said earlier that you can either try to achieve instant smiles, or you can go the extra mile and create a team culture, which generates consistent, if not instant, smiles. So, let me give you an appetizer of what my S.M.I.L.E.S. leadership philosophy entails.

S is for Synergize

The power to synergize means using your collective and relational strength to bring moving parts together into a greater whole. But what does it take to actually *synergize* an entire vision or even just a team project? What does it take to make 1 + 1 = 10 for everything from a one-time project to your entire company direction? It takes grabbing this vision of synergizing and beginning to stimulate and motivate.

M is for Motivate

The leader as coach is a model I believe in, not just as an athlete, but because this model has been proven effective countless times in the business world as well. The power to motivate is the power to convince your team that excellence and success benefits every individual *and* the whole team, thus creating a safe environment of striving for goals rather than just obeying orders. To successfully motivate, you need to be demonstrating several key qualities.

First, you must be *flexible*. You must learn each person's needs, personality and values and strive to adjust your leadership style to the individual. Second, you must be *relational*. You care about the person as a whole, who matters as a human being, not just as an employee who performs a service. Third, you must be *affirming*. Your team needs to know you highly value their work and understand the key component each team member brings to the table. Finally, you must be *inspirational*. It is your job as a leader to give hope, to inspire greatness, and to know what motivates each team member. In short, the leader as coach must be the dynamic, vibrant, vigorous fuel that drives motivated team members to develop, excel and perform at a high level. The leader who attempts to motivate without vital human connections to the team will ultimately fail, but the leader who motivates by inspiring excellence from within will succeed.

I is for Impact

By now, you have created a spirit of curiosity in which your team has been given the vision that a synergistic approach will provide optimal success and satisfaction. You have created a shared direction through your efforts to *synergize*, you have *motivated* the team to do more than they thought they could, and now you are looking to 'turn the light on' in your team's heart—that belief that what they do for the company has significance and that lives are literally changed because of the team effort being launched. Your goal is to create an *impact* on the team members, the team as a whole, the company as a whole, the *industry* as a whole, and even the broader community. Now that synergy is introduced, the motivating principle that synergy is better than individualism is awakened, and *impact* is now clearly seen as an effort-multiplying ingredient, it only remains to flip the switch, in order to lead the way.

L is for Lead

A good leader steps forward hoping he/she will be followed, but a *great* leader establishes "S.M.I." (Synergize, Motivate, Impact) before taking that first step forward knowing their team will be an effective unit. Now you have taken what burns in your own heart and transferred that sense of urgency to your team. They will love what you love and will work at your passion as if it was their own. Now your team, with a new synergy, will surprise you and delight you with the way they pour their souls into each project, as if they thought of it themselves. They are looking forward to the gratifying result of not only seeing a positive team result, but also enjoying the personal satisfaction of being an integral part of something bigger than themselves.

KEVIN DALEY

E is for Empower

As you begin to see your team synergizing, you will come to a crossroads. You can either say, "If it ain't broke, don't fix it" and continue to lead in the same fashion that brought success in your first synergized project together—or you can become an elite leader and say, "If I give more trust to my team, they will achieve even more than if I stay involved at the same level as before." In other words, team success should not just be defined as achieving the same repeatable results under your leadership; it should be defined as achieving *improving* results as an outcome of your *decreased* input. The team players have learned their roles well and, because they are highly motivated, are now bringing their own creative juices and systems to the table. And when you as the elite leader hold a loose rein on your team of stallions, they will run faster.

This is precisely how the Harlem Globetrotters each and every year can hold the attention of hundreds of thousands of fans in their world tours: they continue to develop, grow, change and reformulate. Yes, you see some of the tricks that are trademark Globetrotter—like one of my favorites, the bucket of water—but the organization is *not* merely micromanaged by one man telling all the players precisely what to do. The players bring their own unique twists and talents to the court and these are highly encouraged to be developed and used. And what is the result?

When I was allowed to bring my own sense of shifty fun to the equation, I— as a 6'5" professional athlete—*also* brought a child-like joy to the simple act of sneaking up on an opposing player to play a trick on him, to be immediately followed up by a well-choreographed team effort to score. When I was allowed to be fully myself while in the context of understanding the bigger team objectives, it was then that I was at my very best. In fact, that was the key to my 10-year success.

Your team will be no different. When your team members each understand what it is they excel at, are acknowledged for it *and* are allowed to run like the wind in those areas, then everyone will benefit. And when everyone is benefiting, what do you get? Smiles, of course!

S is for Smile

Okay, *now* is the time for the team celebrations and the fun outings together! Because what you are reveling in and celebrating is a mutual achievement that the team has accomplished together. But more importantly, your team didn't arrive at this point with begrudging get-through-it attitudes. They arrived in unity, with teamwork, and a sense of internally satisfying gratification—the kind of gratification which says, "Okay, what's next? and How can we do it *better*?"

Now you haven't just created a great team effort, you have literally given a gift to your team. In a world in which pain and heartache is inevitable, and in which often my work is just a job and my job is just work, you have helped bring meaning back into the careers and skills of the members of your team. You made getting up on Monday *more* exciting than finishing on Friday afternoon. You made weekends valuable for re-energizing before Monday rather than recovering from yet another week of life that your team members forfeited just to make a paycheck. The trust you have now built into your team is golden, and the next time you want to lead them into battle, they will follow without hesitation.

So, if you're ready to rethink leadership—to make 1 + 1 = 10—and jumpstart the effectiveness of those around you, it's time to start smiling!

Chapter One:
Synergize

"The strength of the team is each individual member. The strength of each member is the team."- Phil Jackson

As a younger man, I got to do something few ever experience: *I got to literally be someone else.* I was selected to participate in one of the most memorable television commercials in recent history when I played a 23-year-old Michael Jordan (of Chicago Bulls fame) against the real 39-year-old Michael Jordan who was currently playing for the Washington Wizards. I was the "body" of the younger Jordan, and the special effects artists then digitally superimposed Jordan's face onto mine. But make no mistake, the basketball we played was very real; we literally played one-on-one against each other for three days.

Since I was supposed to look and play like Jordan, I had to prepare. Since MJ was my favorite player of all time, I had already studied his game quite a bit, but the night before shooting the commercial, videos of Jordan were brought to my hotel and I spent the whole night watching and re-watching these films. I had to *walk* like Michael, *dribble* like Michael, and perform several of his iconic moves. For example, his classic dribbling between his legs repeatedly before suddenly exploding to the baseline against the Boston Celtics' Larry Bird was something I had to perfect. And on top of all that, I had to *dunk* like Michael Jordan. Honestly, at first I was hesitant to play my hardest against him, but when he dunked on *me*, I decided to bring out my best Michael Jordan dunk. Briefly, I remembered my first dunk on a regulation-height basket. I was in the eighth grade playing on an outdoor concrete court with the typical neighborhood chain net. And now I was going head-to-head against the greatest athlete in the world. And I *dunked* on Michael Jordan *as* Michael Jordan. Yes, that's right *I* dunked on Michael Jordan.

The final product was amazing. It was Michael Jordan, the *older*, fully knowing the moves of Michael Jordan, the *younger*, and both endeavoring to outplay the other and giving a whole new meaning to the term "self-respect."

The ability to be someone else—to understand the viewpoint of another in addition to conveying your own vision—is the bedrock key to setting a new and fresher course in your company or team. Just like I studied Michael Jordan so I could *be* Michael Jordan, setting this new direction is the first step in the S.M.I.L.E.S. package: *synergize*. Keep that concept of seeing other viewpoints in mind, and I will return to it shortly.

A Basic Understanding of *Synergize*

The concept of synergy is as old as the Greek language from which this idea originates. Taken from the ancient Greek word *synergos*, which means literally to "together work," to *synergize* is to take advantage of one of the greatest phenomena in the human experience: that several moving parts which work perfectly together create an *output* many times greater than the *input*.

All the way back in 1935, psychologist Kurt Koffka observed famously that "the whole is something else than the sum of its parts."[iii] This well-known observation is often modified to say that the whole is *greater* than the sum of its parts. But Koffka felt that this was an oversimplification. He considered the whole—the result of the sum of the parts—as having a separate existence from the parts. The whole was something not just *greater*, but completely different.

To synergize means setting up a situation in which your team (the "parts") creates an output, which seems to defy any attempt to reverse engineer how something so great resulted. But what is the foundation of this synergy? It is all in how you set up your vision for your team or group and this involves the tremendous skill of learning to be someone else, learning to give a voice to your team until *your* vision is *their* vision and *their* vision is your vision. It means taking the time to listen and learn to produce a direction that everyone can get behind.

The Short Version: How to Synergize

In case you are one who skips to the end of movie to see what happens, let me start with the short version of what it means to synergize—to create a team dynamic going forward which lends itself to greatness and high productivity. The short version is that you have a very simple choice: you can either issue marching orders, or you can gain a directed, meaningful consensus based on listening to others. The first one is faster, but contains much more risk of failure. The second takes much more time and effort, but carries the promise of long-term return on your time investment.

When I was with the Harlem Globetrotters, we always had to work as a team to perform our complicated plays on the court. We made it look spontaneous, but in fact these plays were practiced hundreds of times and calculated down to the second. I would throw the ball to an empty spot on the court, and by the time the ball arrived, the next player was there and already passing to the next empty spot on the court until we ended with a spectacular dunk or trick shot. If *one* guy was out of step, the whole play fell apart and the whole team would look bad. We had to build a consensus that all of us abided by and agreed upon. So, the short of it is: are you an order giver or a consensus builder?

Now, make no mistake; I'm not talking about the type of consensus in which all the best ideas get watered down for the sake of getting along. I'm talking about consensus in which the best of the best thoughts and thinkers are combined into your original vision to give ownership of and excitement to your direction. This is to *synergize*. Let's roll up our sleeves and walk through this process step-by-step.

Synergize Step 1: Vision Definition (Not Idea-of-the-Month)

Remember, the need to synergize is not so much an action step as it is laying the framework and foundation for an upcoming plan of action. To explain the need to synergize, I'm going to lay out a five-step outline of what it looks like to synergize—to set your team up for movement forward. Each step includes a warning of what *not* to do.

Idea-of-the-Month

Let me address the negative warning first. Many leaders call themselves visionaries simply because they have a lot of ideas. They may be creative, yet that does *not* make them visionaries *or* effective leaders. A leader who has what he believes is a terrific idea on a Friday afternoon, and by Monday morning is making announcements about it to his team *may* be a genius, but in many cases is probably just overly impressed with himself.

And when idea after idea fails to gain traction or fizzles over time, that leader often becomes very good at what I might call the "failure spin." The failure spin is the ability to take a leadership failure and try to define it in positive terms for the sake of saving face, a move that almost everyone sees through. Yet the unspoken expectation is that the team members are supposed to just buy into the explanations and scapegoats for failure and wait for the next biggest "idea of the century" to come along in the next few weeks.

This type of leadership brings division, cynicism and a whole lot of resumés being emailed out over lunch hours. That sort of leader is seen as a buffoon and not taken seriously. This can be a problem with small or mid-size company owners who have stopped getting meaningful feedback from anyone. That type of leader tends to simply get rid of people who disagree with him. So, to get the next paycheck, the team hangs on, whispering in the break rooms about the boss and hoping to find a better opportunity.

There is a better way, a way that takes discipline, humility, and patience: vision definition.

Vision Definition

The true visionary—and that is *you* if you choose to be one—is the one who may in fact have many good ideas but is—make a note of this—wise enough *to keep it to themselves until it is more refined.* In other words, the *only* appropriate place for your great ideas is right between your ears and in your own personal notes until it is properly vetted and developed in your own mind.

If you are one who tends to be creative and can see something where nothing yet exists, just caution yourself that for every 10 ideas you have, *maybe* one of them is worth keeping and considering. Let me give you two great tools to define your vision… your next fabulous idea + time and focus.

First, you need time. Your mind needs hours and maybe days to percolate on this vision. Great vision never happens in little pieces of thinking—it happens in sometimes-frantic hours of brainstorming and realizations and exploration of possibilities. If you think you have hit the one-in-a-million idea, then you *must* carve out time to develop it into a meaningfully streamlined structure.

Second, you need focus. To put it simply, *get out of your office!* Your workplace—unless you work in a national forest—is probably the single *worst* place to develop vision. Get away to a peaceful locale and set yourself up to let your brain release normal day-to-day responsibilities so that it can focus exclusively on this direction. And you need some method to take what is *in* your mind and get it *outside* of your mind where you can literally see it and begin to edit yourself. You can use an old-school notebook, or if you prefer electronic methods, organizational programs such as OneNote or EverNote are fabulous.

For me, my time and focus happens at the gym. Although there are many distractions there, for some reason that is where my best ideas happen. I usually get some stimulus by watching YouTube videos on the subject I'm pondering and whenever something vital comes to mind, I make a note on EverNote right from my phone, all while working out.

In 1994, a guy named Jeff Bezos used the tools of time and focus. He took the time to make a cross-country road trip from New York to Seattle. And on this trip he focused and formulated his dream, now the world's largest internet sales company, Amazon. A few days in a car literally changed the way the world shops.

How do you know when you are finished with this process? The answer is: when your vision is clear, succinct, and can literally be expressed in a purpose statement, such as Amazon's vision: *"To be Earth's most customer-centric company, where customers can find and discover anything they might want to buy online."* Since every single person reading this book uses Amazon, I'd say that vision is being fulfilled.

Just to get you started thinking, here are some vision statements of well-known organizations that are the product of *time* and *focus,* which translated into a *synergized* team effort:

- Southwest Air: "To become the world's most loved, most flown, and most profitable airline."
- IKEA: "Our vision is to create a better every-day life for many people."

- Nike: "Bring inspiration and innovation to every athlete* in the world. (*If you have a body, you are an athlete.)"
- Alzheimer's Association: "A world without Alzheimer's disease."
- Nerdster: "To be a nerd for all your needs."
- American Express: "We work hard every day to make American Express the world's most respected service brand."
- Google: "To provide access to the world's information in one click."

So, what do you do with this well-refined vision? How do you begin to get buy-in from the people who will make it a reality? How do you start the process of developing the nuts and bolts operations to make realization of the vision happen?

Synergize Step 2: Personal Connection (Not Bombshell Announcements)

Now your personal excitement over this vision has increased because you believe in it, and have invested time to vet this vision properly. And by the way, it may be that in your time away at your secret headquarters, you came to the conclusion that this was the *dumbest* idea you've ever thought of, so you came home and reset with no one any the wiser! But assuming you are fully on board with your own idea, you now have two choices. Again, I start with the negative warning.

Bombshell Announcements

It *may* be that your team has *so much* faith in you that you can simply walk into a team meeting on Monday morning and surprise everyone with a fantastic new vision you developed in recent weeks. If you already know they will all be on board, this means you have successfully synergized enough times in the past that they have trust in you.

But if you strut into the office and announce your vision in a team meeting, or worse—in a company-wide gathering—you are running a huge risk. You are risking the viability of this idea on your ability to communicate and sell it in just a few minutes. Impressions and judgments will be formed during *the first few sentences you utter*, so unless you know you are one of the greatest communicators around, you had better be certain that five minutes after your first words, the whole team is behind you and ready to go to battle on your behalf. That is not, however, the usual reality. When a broad vision or idea is announced publicly, an instant internal vote has taken place, either for or against. And those against it might carry out your wishes, but it won't be with enthusiasm or personal ownership. There is a better way—a *longer* way—but a better way.

Personal Connection

Instead of calling a team meeting or company gathering on Monday morning, you begin to test the waters at an informal interpersonal level. There are numbers of ways to do this, but I will explain a useful track. First, you calmly identify the absolute key person or key people you need to be on board with you. For the sake of example, we'll create a team of 10 with you at the helm and a second-in-command who is your go-to person. Let's call him Jim.

You tell Jim you want to take him to lunch… a *long* lunch. You need to pick his brain about something, a crazy idea you're having about which you want his informal input. Get out of the office, get informal and get interpersonal. This is not an official meeting and therefore the pressure to pull off a huge sell is simply not there.

At this lunch, you tell Jim the result of your vision definition time away. But your message to Jim is *not*, "Like this and support me." Your message to Jim is, "Poke holes in this. Ask questions. Tell me what doesn't work. Tell me how to make this better."

And this is the part that requires humility and the willingness to be a team player. If Jim feels truly empowered to be honest and if you begin to get genuine feedback, you can start to gauge Jim's interest level. If he senses you interjecting *his* thoughts into *your* vision, sees you taking copious notes or engaging at a real level, Jim will likely begin to own this himself, even while playing devil's advocate.

The end of this time consists of the simple question: *"Is this idea, adjusted now with your thoughts and input, one that we could get behind together?"* If Jim thinks it needs more development, you *might* have just saved yourself and your team from the aforementioned "idea-of-the-month" syndrome, and can either scrap it or continue developing it. More than likely, Jim will already have enough emotional ownership in the vision to invest some time in another meeting to further elaborate and refine it. Likewise, if Jim says, "I think this thing could really fly. I'm totally all in on this," you *still* ought to, in most cases, resist the urge to immediately take it to the team and do a bombshell announcement. Instead, you determine who else should be brought into the loop at this point. Remember, this is still informal; you haven't "put it all out there" yet. No risk has actually been taken. So, in this same spirit of informality, you and Jim decide to get a third key team member, Sarah, involved.

A couple of days later, over some great food at a local hangout, you meet with Jim and Sarah. You *and* Jim present your now-refined vision for a few minutes. Like your meeting with Jim, your message to Sarah is, "Poke holes in this. Ask questions. Tell us what doesn't work. Tell us how to make this better." *But did you notice a key difference?* You are *already* synergizing because you're now asking Sarah for real honest input to help *US (you and Jim)*. In other words, Sarah is already giving input to a mini-team. And yet *still* there is no risk of making a fool of yourself or worse, presenting an idea not developed enough to fly.

Again, with Sarah, you and Jim take the time to *informally* dream and tweak and have fun with this possibility. And this is all based on personal connections. So now, a major transition takes place. And this is a transition that you agree upon together with Jim and Sarah: the time to bring the whole team into the loop.

Synergize Step 3: Gaining Momentum (Not Treading Water)

Jim and Sarah now have contributed buy-in. This is no longer just *your* vision; it is *our* vision. Your final meeting—still informal—consists of developing a winning strategy to present this vision to the other members of the team. Preferably, you are going to include Jim and Sarah in this presentation. And this is where you could get bogged down if you aren't careful.

Treading Water

Your initial presentation to the rest of the team must be *aimed* at an endpoint, and that endpoint, given that you have Jim and Sarah completely on-board with a vision all three of you own, is inviting your team to enter the process of owning it as well. If this initial presentation ends with, "*Well, guys, we just wanted to tell you about this and give you some time to think about it*," you will likely simply have to repeat the same essential meeting all over again. It's possible to get bogged down at this stage and begin talking it to death without actually moving forward. There is a better way: start gaining momentum.

Gaining Momentum

At the end of this initial presentation, let the team know you want some brief, immediate feedback, but that their input will be brought to the table after they've have a short time to process everything. Here is the irony: to gain momentum, you need to allow the team to percolate on your vision long enough to meaningfully contribute. While you don't want to simply keep having discussions that aren't aimed at anything, neither do you want or should you expect to have the initial presentation and a plan to move forward happen at the same time.

Instead you let them know in no uncertain terms—again letting Jim and Sarah affirm their valuable input into the vision—that this vision is far from perfected; you will need the team for this. You send them home, telling them to start putting together their thoughts and that the next meeting will be one in which they now participate in the brainstorming process.

And you are *still* in the informal progression of just floating an idea forward that you may or may not be married to. The more pliable and flexible your vision feels to the team, the more excited they will be to have some meaningful contribution to the overall effort.

Synergize Step 4: Causing Input (Not Manipulated Leader-Pleasing)

Your first team brainstorm session can go one of two ways, and sometimes this direction is subtly hinted at rather than stated openly. It can either be an *actual* team process or it can be a *sham* team process.

Manipulated Leader-Pleasing

When you ask, "What do you think?" does your team take that to mean, "I truly want real thinking and criticism"? Or, does it *really* mean, "Stroke my ego by telling me what a genius idea I have." If you are prone to get angry or at least irritated when a team member disagrees with you, you must take a long look in the mirror and decide whether you are going to really *synergize* or just *demoralize*.

This is a hard possibility to face, but sometimes it's best just to rip the Band-aid off, so here it goes: You may be unaware of the subtle pressure you might be putting on team members to please you, not out of loyalty and affection, but out of fear. Perhaps it's nothing as drastic as fear of job loss or demotion, but fear of the emotional strain that happens when they disagree with you, that they may be treated differently or banished to the proverbial doghouse for a while.

So, in this all-team meeting or series of meetings, instead of engendering the usual leader pleasing, you must authentically invite and encourage real meaningful input.

Causing Input

If you are even slightly wondering if you have succumbed to a manipulated leader pleasing approach, this is the time to assure your team that while you, Jim, and Sarah initially presented this vision, it's now time to consider making it the team's vision. And in a current generation in which even the lowest level employee—whether you agree with this or not—expects to have a voice at some level, giving them that voice can prove extremely beneficial and increase their natural motivation.

Now, as you are brainstorming together, *this* is when you get to do what I did with Michael Jordan: *be someone else*. You have to get into the minds of the team members giving input—ask questions and have *others* ask questions. This stage can and should be messy, filled with rabbit trails and "what if" scenarios. Coffee, snacks and focused uninterrupted time all mixed together is what is needed to look at every facet of your vision, tear it to shreds, put it together again and build a *team* vision.

Here are some good exploratory questions to ask, for example, about one facet of the vision:

- What makes this a direction/procedure/process that works?
- What are possible fatal flaws?
- What would make it fail?
- Is this a good idea or a great idea? Why?
- Can it be streamlined and made more efficient?
- Do we have the capability of making this happen?

- If we don't, is it a great enough idea to *create* the capability?
- What are 3–5 reasons why we might get behind this facet?
- Is anyone here especially excited about this part? Why?
- Is anyone here especially *cautious* about this part? Why?
- Do any of you desperately want to say something but have kept it to yourself so far?
- What are the potential long-range benefits of implementing this vision?
- What are the potential long-range problems if we *do not* implement this vision?

At some point, early in the exploding days of the Internet, Toys R Us must have had similar meetings, but the right questions were *not* asked. They did not have the vision to see that they must have an online presence to be relevant in the growing stay-at-home shopping trend. Instead of asking these vital questions, especially about the potential consequences of *not* changing with the times, they simply outsourced all their online purchases to Amazon. And now Toys R Us is *gone*. This is solely the fault of leadership that did *not* get input from a team. That smells a lot like leadership that makes arbitrary or least unilateral decisions without using the best and brightest they have for vision development.

Let me warn you: the final direction you set as a team will and *ought* to achieve the exact goal you originally aimed for, -- *how* that goal is achieved might look radically different than you expected --but this is what it means to *synergize*! To grow and develop *individual* thoughts and ideas into one unified direction that has fingerprints on it from every team member.

Now that the messes have been made—the ideas floated and shot down, then reassembled with better parts—your leadership instincts must kick in to decide on a key moment: the moment to take the results of your meetings and *move forward* now with an action plan. And this is a key intersection, the time when you take the temperature of your team.

Synergize Step 5: Team Consensus (Not Dictator-Like Pressure)

All the facets of the vision have now been dissected and examined. At this point, it's time to say that the exploratory phase is over and now the team is going to weigh in on a specific direction. And again, I start with the negative warning to avoid blowing the momentum at this juncture.

Dictator-Like Pressure

Yes, you are the leader and yes, this was your original vision. But if after all the painstaking effort to get Jim, Sarah and your team on board you simply push the team to do it your way *anyway*, that team will now have trust issues with you. And this is not a fantasy scenario; some leaders are simply so self-focused that they truly believe they have engaged in a team-building process and then just do everything their way anyway and are *flabbergasted* when anyone suggests that they didn't listen. This is a good way to increase company turnover rates very quickly.

So, if you examine the final direction and it has some input that is different from your original vision, that's a *good* sign. This means you've incorporated the best crème de la crème ideas of your team into the vision and have made it a powerhouse direction that *everyone* can be proud of. Now is the key moment to *synergize:* the moment when the team expresses consensus.

Team Consensus

Again, this consensus of a direction and vision is not built upon the least common denominators that everyone can agree upon. It is built on taking every *good* idea and shattering them in favor of *great* ideas. It is built on working and reworking (see coffee and snacks again!) until the team sits back literally *in awe of the direction that lies before them*. And they *own* it!

This is the time when you now do two things with your team. First, you bring to them a summary definition of what they have come up with and make sure all of them agree that this is what has been discussed. And second, you go one by one to each team member and give them one more chance to express themselves concerning this detailed vision.

Now, it may be that in this second step one team member or two says, "This looks great, but I'm still concerned about that fourth step. I think there's a potential for catastrophic failure which could compromise the whole direction." At that point, remember that if you value your team, if you see them as a gift for the greater good, you will see this moment also as a gift. And this is where your gut instincts as a leader will have to serve you. Because, obviously, sometimes we work alongside people who are just generally negative—they see the cow patty in every beautiful meadow and the fear in every opportunity. At some point, you must decide if that person is useful to your team. Mediocre team members default to "we can't" while great team members say, "It looks challenging, but let's make it happen."

If you are confident in your team and one or two express skepticism or doubt about a piece of the vision at this point—they may be provide a safety valve to prevent a disaster later. Thus, it's worth the time and effort to work through those doubts and get positive ideas to shore up any weaknesses. Every great leader surrounds himself with people unafraid to disagree with him. Once this has been done, and you have now gone member-to-member and gotten their buy-in for this vision as they've formulated it, this is where the fun begins!

President Ronald Reagan kept a plaque on his desk in the Oval Office of the White House. It said, "There is no limit to what a man can do or where he can go if he does not mind who gets the credit." And now that you have accomplished the hard work to *synergize*, your team can move forward and your leadership role is now to get behind the team to the "M" of S.M.I.L.E.S., *motivate*.

Chapter Two:
Motivate

"Motivation is the art of getting people to do what you want them to do because they want to do it." - Dwight D. Eisenhower

What motivates you? What drives your passion for what you do? It might be easy to answer this question for yourself, but if you are going to take the work you've done to *synergize* to the next level, you must be able to answer that question for your whole team. You need to be able to look around the conference room table and give a 5-minute talk about the heartbeat, passion, and personality of every member on your team. In my athletic career, the best coaches I ever had were always the ones with the power to motivate based on their assessment of my skills, my strengths and weaknesses, my own desires and my potential. Great coaches could have a team meeting and be able to articulate that player "A" plays hard to get a scholarship, whereas player "B" is playing because he's trying to make his dad proud, but player "C" was always told he wasn't good enough and he wants to prove his critics wrong. And the coach taps into those motives and reminds each individual that he is behind them. This is where great coaches and great leaders in the business community show their leadership genius: their ability to *motivate*.

I believe with all my heart in the leader-as-coach model when it comes to motivation. I want to give you two key pieces of information to get you on track and motivate your team now that you have *synergized*. First, I want to give you four vital qualities of a motivating leader. Second, I want to encourage you with two vital results your motivating leadership will produce.

Four Vital Qualities of a Motivating Leader

The power to motivate is the power to convince your team that excellence and success benefits every individual *and* the whole team, thus creating a safe environment of striving for goals rather than just obeying orders. But motivating is more than just a great pre-game speech or pre-production speech. To successfully motivate, you must demonstrate four vital qualities. You must be flexible, relational, affirming and inspirational.

You Must be Flexible

Anyone in leadership knows that for certain things you set a standard, which you expect all the team members to follow. If you expect them to be ready for action at 8:00AM sharp, then that is a reasonable expectation. If you set your weekly strategy meeting time at the same time each week, it is fair to expect perfect and consistent attendance at this meeting. I'm not talking about being flexible in the basic structures of how your organization operates. *Total* flexibility would create chaos and hurt your efforts.

What I *am* talking about is being flexible according to three areas of your team members' make-up and constitution. First, you must be flexible with their personality. One team member might be a more sensitive type who needs to talk things through one-on-one to be on board. But since that person brings talents to the company and to your vision, then you can either insist that the team member "get on board" without flexing with his distinct need to process, or you can spend that little bit of extra time with him. He can think aloud, express concerns, and relieve any anxiety he has. On the other hand, another team member might bristle at the prospect of having to verbally process everything on the planet and thinks more in bullet points and marching orders. She might feel oppressed if you had to have a long individual conversation like you did with the first team member. So, with her, you are a little more succinct and to the point; whereas, with the first person you are careful to make sure everything has been talked through adequately.

Second, you must be flexible with their strengths. Trust me, if you find out the two best things each of your team members can do and give them every opportunity to exercise those gifts, to run like a stallion with a loose hand on the reins, you will create *productive* and *happy* employees. They will say, "My leader *gets* me. He *knows* me." Because team members are always the most productive when allowed to run with their biggest strengths, they feel appreciated and understood.

Third, you must be flexible with their weaknesses. One of the biggest leadership mistakes newer leaders make is being overly critical of innate weaknesses in their team members. For example, one team member may be a thinker and visionary who can think at a 35,000-foot level—but has trouble remembering to answer his emails and doesn't check his voicemail half the time. You can either bang your head against the wall trying to correct his weaknesses, or you can just get the genius a personal assistant who will double his effectiveness by making sure he is engaged in *thinking* and not in mundane details that are elusive to him. In other words, if you come alongside and *help* shore up weaknesses, rather than just berating or giving poor job evaluations based on weaknesses, you will increase team effectiveness *and* stop fighting a battle that doesn't have to be fought. *Be flexible!*

In 2001, I had the opportunity to play professional basketball in Lebanon, but my game began to suffer. This was not because of lack of talent or ability on my part, but because I was being put in a situation that ignored my strengths, tried to make me rely on my weaknesses, and did not fit my playing style. My entire playing life, I played the shooting guard and small forward positions, but the team was putting me in as a point guard. I gave it 110% but was not succeeding because the coach did not flex with me. I believe that had he known my playing style, put me predominantly where I was strongest, and found great players to play where I was weaker, we could have had a dynamic powerhouse team.

You Must be Relational

I am constantly amazed that some leaders will try to fool their team members into thinking that they really care by using relationship techniques such as remembering a spouse's name, children's names, and asking how their weekend was. But generally speaking, people will begin to see through this approach and think, "Oh, he must have learned these things at the "Relational Leadership" seminar he went to last year."

Those things aren't inherently bad, but there is a simple key question to ask yourself: *"Am I using techniques and habits to give the impression that I care about my team, or do I genuinely care for them as human beings and as people beyond just employees who achieve goals for me?"* You absolutely must be honest with yourself about this. Sure, you can decide to stay detached, to not let emotion be a part of your working world. After all, you *are* a professional, right? Or, you can decide to be vulnerable and to genuinely care about your team members, to not just learn an employee's husband's name, but to know that he had a bout with cancer a couple years back and they are hopeful he is clear, but not sure yet… To know that the quietest team member you have used to be a professional singer and still thinks about that dream on occasion… To know that one team member has four kids going to college in the next six years and needs to be part of a successful lucrative team effort.

I don't care if you are in a metropolitan culture like New York or Los Angeles, or a suburban bedroom community or a rural setting, the relational leader knows that sometimes a backyard barbeque is an integral part of the team-building process. I'm not talking about the cliché official company Christmas party that is a token of semi-heartfelt gratitude. I'm talking about an informal time where you and your team have the chance to just hang out and remember that you are working with human beings, to meet each other's spouses and children. Sometimes softball, a good meal, Ultimate Frisbee, bowling, chips and salsa, or basketball is a key investment that pays dividends later.

Now, this might go against some conventional wisdom you have heard. Certainly, if you have hiring and firing power over your team, you can't be as close to them as you are with personal friends. You still need to be able to confront and even discipline underperformance. But, neither does this mean you can't genuinely demonstrate care and concern for each team member as an individual. One helpful article which addresses this balance states, "Your relationship with your people should be driven by neither control nor friendship, defined by neither affection nor authority, though affection and authority should certainly be pieces of the puzzle."[iv] So, while you maintain your position as leader, you *can* still be relational.

But again—you *cannot* just start doing things that *look* relational. You must decide to genuinely care about each member of your team. And if you will emotionally invest in them, they are more likely to emotionally invest in your vision.

You Must be Affirming

Your team needs to know you highly value their work and understand the key component each team member brings to the table. In the relational element of motivation, you are caring for the team as human beings. In the *affirming* element, you are caring for them as competent professionals. It is imperative to affirm their professional goals, their greatest skills, their positive *and* negative feedback, and their thought processes.

First, you ought to affirm their professional goals. Do you know what every team member is aiming towards? Can your vision help them personally achieve this through causing growth in the company? If a team member believes that he or she is just a rung on the ladder of *your* career, you probably won't get much out of them. But, if he/she believes you want to be a rung on the ladder of *his/her* career, you will get loyalty and performance.

Second, it is vital to affirm their greatest skills. Are you willing to give public praise for someone else's fabulous work, which takes the spotlight off yourself? Are you willing to view team members as the real experts in their particular areas of responsibility, or do you have to appear to be the only real expert? Every great leader knows instinctively to surround himself with quality people who bring more to the table than the leader can personally bring in every needed subcategory.

Third, you must affirm positive *and* negative feedback. If a team member is confident she can not only tell you what she thinks is working, but can also express concern or alternative viewpoints, then that is an affirmed team member who feels part of a team. And the affirmed team member who is willing to respectfully disagree with you is acting in *your* best interest by helping you avoid possible mistakes, which hamper the vision.

Finally, you ought to affirm their thought processes. Not only do you affirm feedback you receive, but the wise leader also will pick that team member's brain to find out how she arrived at that conclusion. For example, a team member might bring up, "Hey, I don't think this distribution plan is going to work. It will cost more than it will benefit us." You *could* say, "Thanks for the input, but we're going to stick with this plan." That would be sort of okay, but more effectively, you ought to say, "Help me understand your thinking. Prove your point to me, and then we'll reexamine it." *Everyone* benefits from affirming thought processes!

KEVIN DALEY

You Must be Inspirational

Business Insider recently published a diagnostic checklist for team leaders doing some introspection on leadership styles. In addressing motivation, they gave good insight that leaders require effort from their team, but not to the point of unrealistic perfectionism. The author states,

> Great leaders demand—and *inspire*—employees to work hard. They lead by example and give workers the tools they need to succeed through hard work. Bosses who are too rigid are simply unrealistic. People make mistakes. It happens. If you punish small failures, you'll just stifle innovation, experimentation and proactivity in your office.[v]

Your team must have the expectation of success but the freedom to fail. The freedom to fail is ironically the key to success. Just ask Thomas Edison (10,000 tries before inventing a successful light bulb), or my all-time favorite basketball player, Michael Jordan, whose early coaches felt he didn't have the minimum height or skills to truly be great. Jordan even famously said in a Nike advertisement, "I've missed more than 9,000 shots in my career; I've lost almost 300 games. Twenty-six times, I've been trusted to take the game winning shot and missed. I've failed over and over and over again in my life. And that is why I succeed."

What does it mean, then, to be *inspirational*? For those of you who do not have naturally outgoing life-of-the-party personalities, never fear. You don't have to grow a new temperament overnight. In fact, introverts can be some of the best leaders because they are often creative; they listen well; and, they work well in a crisis. For example, arguably one of the most successful businessmen in history, Warren Buffett, is a self-described introvert. He studies. He ponders. He listens. He invests. He creates success. So, no, you don't have to instantly develop the personality of a loud politician.

But like Buffett, you can use your own personality to the fullest to inspire others. I met Warren Buffett when he attended a Harlem Globetrotters game in his hometown in Nebraska. He came to the locker room, and when we were about to have a picture taken together, he said, "Act like you're taking my wallet!" We both laughed and bonded in that one moment. Though he describes himself as an introvert, with that one statement, he created comfort, fun, joy and relationship. I never forgot that incident because *that* is inspirational!

I will define what it means to be inspirational in one short sentence: *It is the ability to give hope.* Hope is often the only difference between success and failure. The mere belief that you *can* do something is often the driving force behind accomplishing that goal. And this has nothing to do with having the ability to give a locker room speech. Yes, hope can be given in a team meeting in which you loudly tell them that this vision *is* achievable and *is* do-able. But hope can also be given with a quiet, "Brandon, I believe in you. You are the right person for this task."

Hope is what has inspired great acts of heroism in times of war. Hope is what has inspired great athletic achievements. And, hope is what has inspired great feats of accomplishment in the business community. As of the writing of this book, doing a Google search for "I have a bad boss" will yield almost 23 *million* results. And a search for "My boss gives me hope" returns only just over 1 million results—and most of the top hits are still negative. In other words, there is a vacuum of hope and inspiration. There are millions of people wishing they had a leader who would care for them enough to inspire them.

One team member said this of his first supervisor: "He had this magic where he could just make you feel like you could do absolutely anything. He instilled confidence like no one I've ever known . . . he really had a way of making you feel like you were part of a team. He knew what you did mattered. It mattered to the company and it mattered to him.'"vi

Your determination to motivate your team by being flexible, relational, affirming and inspirational is absolutely vital to the success of your vision. You have *synergized* the team, but that extra level of inspiration now becomes the difference between putting unleaded gasoline or *rocket fuel* in their tanks! And because of your efforts to *motivate*, there are some vital results you should expect.

Two Vital Results of a Motivating Leader

Your Team Gets Addicted to Success

Once you have motivated your team and they begin to experience success at a level that is new to them, they will essentially get addicted to this feeling of achievement and want to repeat it. All great leaders and team players love the feeling of achieving something outstanding. This is what drives the team to push even *harder* for the next project or vision.

NFL quarterback John Elway played his entire career with the Denver Broncos. Arguably one of the greatest quarterbacks in the history of the game, Elway's specialty was motivating his team to come back from behind to win, leading 35 fourth-quarter comebacks in his career. In the first 14 years of his career, he led his team to the Super Bowl three times, but could never quite get the win. But at the age of 37, he led Denver to victory in the Super Bowl, and speculation was that this would be a great way to end his career. After all, 15 seasons as a record-holding future Hall of Fame quarterback is enough, right? Not for Elway. He came back to win a *second* Super Bowl. Why? Because like all great leaders and team players, he *loved* the feeling of achieving something impossible and unattainable. He had done it once and wanted to do it again.

Following the victory parade after winning the Stanley Cup, the first championship for a Washington, DC team in 26 years, one of the Capitals hockey players, T.J. Oshie, suggested a brand new chant to their massive crowd of fans: "Back to back!"

When your team begins to operate as a *synergized* and *motivated* team, they will relish the next opportunity for success... to be the "dream team" of the company under your leadership.

Your Personal Reputation Elevated

Dirk Koetter, head coach of the Tampa Bay Buccaneers, didn't just walk into the front office of an NFL franchise and receive a job. He coached at the high school level and led teams to greatness. He then worked his way through offensive coordinator jobs at five different colleges before becoming head coach at Boise State where he enjoyed tremendous success. Everywhere he went the teams got better. And yet he never personally made a single play on the field with any of the teams he coached. He was the life, the training and the motivation *behind* the great things that happened. The Tampa Bay Buccaneers didn't go after all the great *players* that Koetter coached—they wanted the coach!

The irony in this -- is when you as the team leader create a great team, although you may be in reality in the background directing and inspiring the team, that ultimately it is *your reputation,* which will be enhanced and will benefit you personally. When the *team* does well, the *leader* gets the credit. And while you, the leader-as-coach, will rightly give credit to the team, the team and those the team impacts will give credit to *you* and appreciate and even love *you* for what *you* did. Why? Without you, the vision would *not* have existed, the direction would *not* have been set, and the courage to break new ground would *not* have been present. Trust me, team members want a leader they can be proud of and for whom they would go the extra mile, and the power to *motivate* makes this dynamic a reality.

Chapter Three:

Impact

"Could anything be better than this? Waking up every day knowing that lots of people are smiling because you chose to impact lives, making the world a better place." - Anyaele Sam Chiyson

    You have now put together a vision that will positively influence profits, company image, and future expansion possibilities. The team is excited and motivated. When you give the green light that the vision is a 'go,' great and thrilling things are going to start happening. But now, your job as the team leader is to cast a vision of potential *impact*. This may end up being integrated into your brainstorming meetings, but this component of my S.M.I.L.E.S. formula deserves individual attention. The assessment of potential impact can, in and of itself, provide an even higher level of motivation to the entire team. I want to challenge you to identify three levels of impact that your vision will have. The first one is standard, the second a little more eye opening, and the third is absolutely groundbreaking.

Level One: What is the Impact on the Company?

Obviously, impact on the company is the main reason for your vision in the first place. You want the company to be sound and more effective all around. You want to push ahead of your main competitors. Everyone gets this, but you ought to communicate potential company impact in concrete mind-blowing terms. If your vision will result in a potential .03% increase in sales, that's not even worth getting out of bed to hear. But if your vision could potentially add 25% more quality sales leads to your customer base, then that is an eyebrow-raiser of impact!

I personally know of one visionary—a simple mid-level employee in a fast food chain. Because he naturally understands the concept of *impact*, he personally took it upon himself to try and improve a single process in food preparation. By simply changing the way a particular vegetable was sliced, he gained more useable food from each vegetable. He proved to his managers that this one change in a single process would save the individual store thousands of dollars per year, and when translated to the entire company, this meant *millions* of dollars saved. That employee got the attention of those many levels above him. Why? Because he proved a mind-blowing impact! And, that wasn't even his job! Needless to say, a raise and a promotion happened instantly for this visionary.

Impact on the company makes everyone feel good, especially when the impact on the individual members of the team is also likely. We work in the world's greatest free market economy in which people rightly expect to be rewarded for success. If possible, you ought to build into your impact statement personal rewards for your team members… the result of making the vision a reality. However, just looking at company impact is normal and expected. Let's look the bigger-picture.

Level Two: What is the Impact on the Industry?

Are you just successfully repeating what others have done? Or, is your vision big enough to literally change the industry in which you work?

Will your efforts be observed and then copied by others because of the amazing impact on even basic thought processes in the industry?

For example, there has always been a shortage of organ donors in the United States. The standard procedure has always been to use pre-authorized organs from deceased donors. However, the Wake Forest Institute for Regenerative Medicine recently announced a whole new way of thinking: a 3D printer than can print from live cells entire tissues and organs that are viable for transplant. As of the writing of this book, pre-clinical trials are being performed on this system, which could save countless lives.[vii] *That* team leader is thinking in terms of industry-wide impact!

Yes, innovative companies such as Apple, Amazon, and Google all 'wow' us with their seemingly endless supply of good ideas. But you have a crack team of experts in your field, too. Think bigger and think industry impact, even if it is simply in one little detail. Now, let's think completely outside-the-box. Company impact is expected. Industry impact is amazing. Then, there is one more level of impact that your team can accomplish:

Level Three: What is the Impact on the *World*?

You have established the anticipated *impact* for the company and even industry. But is that all there is? Is the impact within and for the company aimed just at profits, company image, and future benefits? Can you take this *impact* even further?

My time with the Harlem Globetrotters convinced me that *impact* must be more than just about our own organization. Only approximately 10% of our time was spent on the court for our games in front of crowds of thousands. Most of our time was spent on *world* impact. Anything that is done with excellence can be a gateway opportunity to humanitarian love and charity. How can an exhibition basketball team that entertains arenas full of people around the world be an opening to reach out to those in need? At every show we put on—hundreds per year—the team knew that the arena that night would be filled with people excited to have a good time… to enjoy a night out with their family. But we also knew in that crowd would be men, women and children who didn't just want to laugh or be thrilled by great basketball players; they needed hope and encouragement. They needed a healthy dose of courage and faith, and the joy we provided helped them just a little in that endeavor.

At countless times in my decade as the captain of the Harlem Globetrotters, we visited people who needed to feel special: those fighting cancer, children with terrible illnesses and accident victims. I will never forget an e-mail I received from a lady. She told me she was dying in a local hospital, and that her husband insisted on watching one of our games on T.V. She refused, saying she didn't like basketball and didn't want to watch the game. Her husband kept prodding her to watch the game until she finally agreed. She wrote me to thank me for bringing joy and laughter into her life for the moments she watched me. She said it made her feel *so* good, and she desperately needed that time.

Even today, though I am retired from the team, I am very proud to be associated with the Harlem Globetrotters because of the unique ability they possess to reach the hearts of the hurting. Just recently, some of my former teammates visited a special 7-year-old battling a rare and aggressive form of cancer. Just the simple act of bringing him his own custom jersey, some Harlem Globetrotters basketball gear, and hanging out with him brought a light to his life he needed badly at that moment.

At an even more organized level, the Harlem Globetrotters reach communities through their major initiatives to prevent bullying, reach out to hospitalized fans, teach character at local schools, and encourage a fitter, more active lifestyle for children.

As a player, I was excited to be a Harlem Globetrotter because *more than any other sports team on earth*, we had and the organization continues to have a platform from which to spread human kindness and cheer. And in the "I" of my own S.M.I.L.E.S. formula, *Impact*, is precisely the goal—for you to bring a smile to your team through the sense of world impact, influence, and satisfaction—that they can achieve through your team vision and direction. How do you do that?

Tapping into the Servant Hearts of Your Team

You have now been able to *synergize* and *motivate*. You have demonstrated potential company and industry impact, but there is one more piece of the puzzle to put into the game plan: the *world impact* that this vision will accomplish. It is now time to add to your vision a greater clarity regarding the humanitarian and philosophical reasons for this vision. Unless you are already a not-for-profit organization, this will be a more challenging part of the process, but one that will plant seeds now to grow into oak trees later. And this is the process of tapping into the servant hearts of your team; the idea that *all the members of your team at a fundamental human level have a desire to do something bigger than themselves*. Let me prove this to you.

Your team might not have a world-wide stage like the Harlem Globetrotters upon which to change lives, but more than likely each of them have a *personal* stage from which they try to make a difference. Someone on your team may volunteer at their local church, another might be a foster parent, and another might visit a local nursing home every Sunday afternoon to play games or visit with residents. Why do they do this? Very simply because they are human, but *also* because it does something for them personally. These actions in which they receive nothing tangible in return, provides for them a sense of personal mission and purpose that they are making a difference that really matters.

I have friends who solicit donations for charitable organizations or not-for-profit educational institutions, and they get to interact every week with financial donors. And what I've learned from them is that asking for money is not really the point; the "ask" as they call it, is the result of something that has already been generated: a need to belong and make a difference. When people who donate $25 or $250,000 are asked why they are doing this, their motivation is often associated with the *feeling* that they get when they donate; that the satisfaction of being part of something big and important thrills the soul and fills the heart. And thus, they continue giving!

Remember that your team isn't just made up of company-benefitting robots to earn a profit; they are human beings with a natural desire for significance. The wise leader will attempt to tap into that desire rather than just seeing their people as money-making machines from Monday through Friday who do charitable things on the weekends. For some of your team members, the charitable things they do on the weekends—if they were being honest—often mean *more* to them than their job, even if they love working on your team.

So, how do you tap into this servant heart that already exists on your team? The vision you have now created with your team by your effort to *synergize* and *motivate* has some icing on the cake to add. You have done the hard work of putting together the nuts and bolts of your vision, the direction you are headed, and how this will benefit the company. But how will it benefit the company and *beyond*? There are literally *so* many possibilities that a whole book could be filled with ideas, but it starts with finding out more about the heartbeat of your people—the tender human side of them that is not about deadlines, projects, meetings and profits.

This is an important enough step with your team, I believe it warrants some time dedicated to this effort to provide *world impact*. This is a time together, whether in one well-run meeting or in a series of meetings, in which you propel your vision to a higher level of meaning. The excellence of the vision has already provided personal excitement for the team as well as potential huge benefit to your organization. You have already identified how this vision will be a game-changer for your own organization. And perhaps you've even built some personal incentives into the program such as bonuses, vacations, or prizes.

But now is the time to look beyond the 'self' and examine the *impact* not just on the company and industry, but on others perhaps even outside the company. And by the way, this direction will obviously have the residual benefit of painting your company in a positive light for the community and your customer base. Those folks *also* have a natural desire to make a difference.

And again, rather than you as the leader just dictating what a difference the team vision will make, this is the time to involve them in the *impact* part of the vision. This a similar process to brainstorming the original vision, but now you are having a meaningful discussion about matters of broader human importance, perhaps even matters of life and death. Let me run through a sample scenario of establishing bigger *impact*.

World Impact Brainstorm Session

You gather your team together and set a tone of importance and value at the beginning, congratulating them on setting a team vision that is going to impact the company and industry, but now you want to talk about how this vision is going to make a human impact. If you are not necessarily gifted at softer personal conversations, then now is the time to step up. Any team member appreciates it when you ask how work is going, but they *really* appreciate it when you ask how a sick mother is getting along or how an autistic child is progressing; they desire personal contact. This is *not* a business meeting where the goal is to get to an endpoint as quickly and efficiently as possible. Here are some great starter questions to get this conversation rolling, remembering that the *process* is as important as the final result.

- Who are the most important people in your lives and why?
- Who has had the biggest personal impact on your life?
- If you were independently wealthy and didn't *have* to work for money, what would you do with your life besides recreation?
- What human needs reach your heart the most?
- Who do you wish you could help?

- Do you have personal situations that have raised awareness of a greater need? (Such as a disabled child or rare disease?)

I'm not talking about setting unrealistic goals such as, "Our team is going to save the planet." I'm talking about do-able goals such as sponsoring a scholarship, underwriting a homeless shelter, raising funds for research of a specific disease, and so forth—things that aren't political in nature and that human beings generally agree upon.

For example, Ethos Water, a subsidiary of Starbucks, achieved all three levels of impact. First, they impacted the company. They are definitely for-profit and have been a good moneymaker for Starbucks. Second, they impacted the industry. They broke new ground in linking their product (water) with their *cause*, which is *also* water. In other words, they sell *water* to benefit their passionate cause, which is access to clean *water*. Which brings me to the fact that third, they achieved *world impact*. Ethos Water, the brainchild of Peter Thum who worked in South African communities that lacked clean water, has now granted millions of dollars to support clean water and sanitation programs.

Life is short, and people want to make a difference. If you can demonstrate to your team that they will experience personal impact (which benefits the company), yield industry-wide impact (which benefits the reputation of the company and the trade as a whole), and create *world* impact in which real lives are changed for the better, now your efforts to move forward have gained tremendous power and momentum.

Now it's time to pull the trigger on the starting gun: it's time to *lead*.

Chapter Four:

Lead

"Leadership is the art of giving people a platform for spreading ideas that work." - Seth Godin

When I first joined the Harlem Globetrotters, I knew of their reputation for having fun, making people laugh, and enjoying a more laid-back sporting atmosphere. After being invited to their headquarters to try out, I was in for a big surprise: the coaching staff worked the new potential members of the team like the NBA finals were coming up next week. I can honestly say the Harlem Globetrotter practices were more grueling and intense that anything I had ever experienced.

Once I made the team, we worked on every single well-coordinated play hundreds of times to perfection. We were intensely coached, and we worked hard at our famous ball-handling skills. We were rigorously drilled at the various humorous routines we put on. Every single facet of our show was broken down, analyzed, corrected, scrutinized and reworked. The word "again" became a regular part of our vocabulary. Every player was expected to bring hard work, extreme discipline and world-class athletic ability. We ran routines and plays so many times, I would *dream* about them and for a few moments not know if I was in my bed or on the court!

The Harlem Globetrotters exhibited leadership to do something no other sports team had ever done: create a high-level athletic experience combined with comedy and laughter for the general benefit of all mankind. Nothing about it was original, but the combination of elements was completely original and groundbreaking. I was so intrigued by this high-level leadership ability that I wanted in on the action. I soon became the team captain and would serve in this capacity for many years. It was exhilarating to me to be able to be part of something that was truly *synergized*. And the lessons I learned each year with the team quickly become part of my D.N.A., part of who I am as a leader. But my role as the captain of the team was an interesting integrated role—meaning that not only did I provide *leadership*, I also had to *perform*. I could *not* lead effectively if my own performance on the court was lackluster or anything short of spectacular. Trust me, I was motivated to stay at the top of my game, so that I had a platform from which to lead others. If I worked to help motivate the team to greatness, and yet I personally was not bringing my absolute best each day, then my leadership would have fallen flat and failed. This is because *followers* will only rise to the level of their *leader*.

You have now created synergy with your team. You have motivated them and you have convinced them of the impact your/their vision can potentially make. Now, it only remains to begin to implement the vision. As you already know, I love acronyms, so we'll let another one guide our thinking on your effort to *lead*: L is for Launch; E is for Exit; A is for Assess; D is for Direct.

L is for Launch

The world is full of dreamers. In fact, having a vision or a dream is part of being human. But the world is *not* full of leaders. A leader is one who can formulate or take a formulated vision and proceed from the *theoretical* to the *actual*. This is a quality that the military looks for in its own leadership. Many great leaders in the business community were first leaders in the military. And one 'must-have' quality that they learned was the ability to pull the trigger—to take a plan of action and implement it. This is an act of balanced self-confidence in which the leader is confident in the plan and able to give the order to execute the plan. Many visionaries have seen their dreams stall because they can't get from the proverbial drawing board to carrying out the plan.

Fortunately for you, you have not made it to where you are today without being able to launch. But even the most seasoned leaders can sometimes falter at the moment of actual execution. This can happen for a host of reasons, like anything from psychological stress from past failures to personal issues such as health or relationship problems. The focus that it takes to say, "Ready—Set—*GO!*" is tremendous, and you must be ready for that moment. And the visionary who is also a great leader must be able to look at the calendar, point to a day and say, "*That one.* That's Day One of the master plan."

The amazing military might have an aircraft carrier rooted in the fact that it carries a small air force on the ship. The ability to launch a state-of-the-art warplane from a deck much shorter than a standard runway takes meticulous detailed planning. The plane is moved into position, the towbar is attached to the launching shuttle, and the holdback bar is also attached. At the same time, the jet blast deflector is raised behind the plane, the flight crew makes all final checks, and the catapult officer readies the catapults from the catapult control pod. He charges the steam pressure level so that it's perfect for the type of plane being launched along with conditions on the deck. Finally, the pilot blasts the engines. At *that* moment, everything is in the hands of the catapult officer. It is up to *him* to pick the right moment to release the catapults, thrusting the plane from 0 to around 165 miles per hour in two seconds flat. Needless to say, the Navy doesn't choose squeamish or indecisive people to be catapult officers. They must possess the courage to launch a 45,000 pound aircraft carrying a human being into the air, an action in which about 3–5 total seconds will determine whether the plane will fly or hit the ocean.

Despite all the confidence you have built in your own mind, and in the mind of your team, there is obvious risk of failure when you finally say, *"GO!"* But ultimately you must decide that you believe in your plan and act accordingly. *You* must launch your plan.

E is for Exit

If you have successfully prepared your team for the launch date, you *must* do the hardest thing for a visionary leader to do: *let go*. When the catapult officer releases a fighter plane from the deck of an aircraft carrier, he cannot get into the pilot's seat and fly the plane. The pilot must do what he has trained to do.

The temptation to think you will ensure the success of your vision by keeping your fingers in every moving part can be overwhelming, but that tendency will doom the project to fail. Your team members can carry out the mandate given to them, but they must be given latitude to accomplish their individual goals in the ways that make the most sense to them. To a certain degree, you must exit the process at this point. You must let the moving parts move.

And there is a positive residual benefit to stepping back and letting your team do their thing: you are showing confidence in them, which turns into positive performance. I believe it is impossible to overestimate the role that self-confidence plays in human performance in any venue. Phenomena such as winning streaks, world records, or upticks on a stock price are all often traced back to confidence levels. Margie Warrell, contributor to *Forbes Magazine*, makes an important observation that, "Confidence is not a fixed attribute; it's the outcome of the thoughts we think and the actions we take… it is not based on your *actual* ability to succeed at a task, but your *belief* in your ability to succeed."[viii]

If, on the other hand, the first thing you do on launch day is start micro-managing every task, you are sending a *GIANT* message to your team that you don't trust them. And their confidence, motivation and performance will all suffer. Therefore, your job on Launch Day is at least partly to keep a fairly low profile—to encourage and motivate, but not to be a back-seat driver. Let your team do what they do best as you exit.

A is for Assess

"Wait a minute, Kevin! You just said to keep a low profile. And now you want me to assess what's happening?" Absolutely, I do because there is a profound difference between micromanaging and providing accountability. The micromanager plays Russian roulette with his team's emotions because they *never* know when or if he will suddenly step in to muddy the waters with over-involvement. But the leader who provides accountability does so in a *predictable* manner than has been pre-set.

For example, in your planning stage, *before* your launch date, you inform your team that there will be an assessment function built into your plan (Key Performance Indicators or KPIs). This assessment is *not* for the purpose of being critical and condescending, but to keep tabs on how you can serve your team. In other words, assessments exist for *their* benefit, which in turn benefits the entire project or vision. An assessment schedule might look something like the following. In this scenario, the team is divided into several sub-teams each working together on a particular key facet of the vision. The boxes with an "X" indicate you are checking in with that person, sub-team, or the entire team together.

Time Frame	Team Members	Sub-Teams	Full-Team
Week 1, Day 1	X		
Week 1, Day 3	X		
Week 1, Day 5		X	
Week 2, Day 1			X

1 *plus one* = TEN

Week 2, Day 3	X		
Week 2, Day 5	X		
Week 3, Day 1		X	
Week 3, Day 5			X
Week 4, Day 1	X		
Week 4, Day 5			X

Now, you can make it perfectly clear this is your check-in schedule. You aren't holding their hands, but neither are you putting on blinders without assessing progress. You can organize this in whatever fashion best suits your needs, but the important thing is that everyone is on the same page regarding assessment. On the days you are not checking in with anyone, keep your low profile and let people work. On the days you *are* assessing, your demeanor is that of being helpful, being a sounding board and providing support.

Now, your assessments are naturally going to yield feedback information that you could not gain in the theoretical planning stage. The reality of the day-to-day operation will help you use these assessments to positive advantage in the final step in leading:

D is for Direct

Based on your assessments, course corrections will likely be necessary. Your team should know this upfront and be ready to help make these modifications. It is up to you to get feedback from your team as to what course corrections will be helpful and which would just be upending the process before you've really built up steam. You make judgment calls (hopefully with as much team member input as possible) as to how to adapt to aspects of the plan that are failing or underperforming, how to overcome unexpected hurdles, or even how to maximize an area that is working *better* than you anticipated.

And this is where all your effort to *synergize* and *motivate* and *impact* come to fruition because your team shouldn't view your directing the ship in a slight course correction as somehow punitive, but as a wise ship captain guiding the crew to the most successful voyage possible. In fact, inside your own head you may be *screaming* for a particular course correction. But before you issue orders, set up your team to make that suggestion themselves. Let the team *own* the course correction rather than it always coming from you. Here are 10 core questions to ask about any particular aspect of your vision to help guide your team to get behind directing in a slightly different path:

1. Is it working, and should we do *more* of it or the *same*?
2. Is it *not* working and should we *stop* doing it or *improve* it?
3. What is going better than you thought?
4. What is going worse than you thought?
5. What is the top one thing you would change about this if you could right now?
6. What it the top one thing you *love* about what is happening right now?
7. What resources do you need to make this course correction? Are they prohibitive?
8. What have you learned about this process you didn't know a week/month/quarter ago?
9. What do I, as the leader, need to better understand about your part in this process?
10. What am I missing? Is there an 'elephant in the room' that needs to be said, but hasn't come up?

From Lead to Empower

If you are successful at your efforts to L.E.A.D.—launch, exit, assess, direct—then you will have essentially already done the hard work of

1 *plus one* = TEN

getting your team to the *empower* part of my S.M.I.L.E.S. leadership formula. They will own this vision, and it will begin to change, grow and improve *whether you direct it to or not*. To *empower* your team will be to simply take the *lead* step to the next longer term level.

Colin Powell, who at the time was the national security advisor to President Ronald Reagan, recalls an incident in which he was in the Oval Office explaining to the president a difficult problem to solve. But during the conversation, Powell noticed that the President was far more interested in the group of cute squirrels that had gathered outside the office. President Reagan was famous for his love for squirrels, and he regularly put acorns outside for them so they would come close. And, to think the President was more interested in the squirrels than he was in the national security problem to be solved! But reflecting on this incident, Powell came to understand that the President had made him national security advisor for a reason: it was *his* job to solve these problems, and with a smile Powell realized that Reagan's interest in the squirrels was a simple way to tell Powell, "I believe in you; I trust you; I have faith in you."[ix]

Your vision is *happening*. Your team is *working*. 1 + 1 = 10 is becoming a *reality*. Your leadership has carefully made certain the dream or project is on course. Now, it's time to think longer-term—to see 1 + 1 = 10 can become $1 + 1 = 10^2$ or 10^3. It's time to *empower*.

Chapter Five:
Empower

"People want guidance, not rhetoric. They need to know what the plan of action is and how it will be implemented. They want to be given responsibility to help solve the problem and the authority to act on it.-"Howard Schultz

The ultimate challenge in the field of power generation is how to create a self-perpetuating power source. The dream of power engineers is to produce a power creation system *that powers itself with the energy it creates.* This is the hope of a theoretical perpetual, motion machine—a machine that could do work forever without an external energy source. Of course, this machine is impossible to create because it would violate some of the most basic laws of physics. Nevertheless, pursuit of this dream continues upon many fronts.

But there is another way to create something *like* perpetual motion: Isaac Newton's First Law of Motion. This law basically says that an object will remain at rest or in uniform motion *unless* an external force changes that state. Or to be down-to-earth (literally), this means that if you let go of a basketball in the air, it will drop because an external force (gravity) is acting on that basketball.

So, let's talk about the difference between an object at rest versus an object with an external force acting on it to change its direction or speed. The object at rest in your world is a vision, which produces one result, one time, or *perhaps* the same result repeatedly. This is not inherently bad and in fact is an indicator that your efforts to *synergize, motivate, impact* and *lead* have been successful. For example, if your vision was to create a net 5% increase in productivity of a manufacturing process and you achieve that goal, it may be your intention to now move on to a completely different vision.

But what if your vision existed not just to achieve a goal once or even to achieve the same result repeatedly, but to gain *momentum* whereby your vision is self-growing and self-developing? What would it take to create a system in which your vision essentially develops a life of its own? If I put this in chart form using the same 5% productivity increase as an example, it would look like this:

Vision	Outcome
Level 1: Achieve 5% productivity increase next year.	The Vision achieves the Goal
Level 2: Achieve 5% productivity increase each year.	The Vision achieves the Goal
Level 3: Achieve 5% productivity increase next year, which creates 6.5% the following year, which creates 8% the year after.	The Vision *CREATES* and *ACHIEVES* more related Goals.

In other words, "Level 1" and "Level 2" are absolutely successful outcomes. Your goals have been achieved; the vision is a success. But then it comes to a stopping point, and you start from scratch on a new vision.

But in "Level 3," your vision has momentum that is self-perpetuating; it takes on essentially a life of its own.

As an example, in 1999, a new company brought to consumers a different way of thinking about photographs: using internet-based image publishing to custom-order photos and photos gifts of all kinds. At first it was relatively unknown, but as customers spontaneously spread the word, this company—Shutterfly—began to take on a life of its own. It went public in 2006 and in recent years has experienced phenomenal growth each year, winning business awards from various ranking organizations. The *Wall Street Journal* even partially credited Shutterfly for an upsurge in the sales of paper products.[x] Other business reporting groups and news agencies such as *SmartMoney*, *USA Today*, *California CEO*, *Macworld*, NBC's *Today Show* and CBS's *Early Show* among many others, have featured the unique service Shutterfly brought to consumers. But it wasn't just dry business articles that featured Shutterfly by giving profit and growth numbers; *Shutterfly met an emotional home and family need for consumers!* And as a result, the company has been featured in *Glamour*, *InStyle*, *Good Housekeeping*, *EliteDecor*, *Haute Living*, *Family Circle* and many other publications, which tap into the innate need to create joy in family life. How did Shutterfly accomplish harnessing this broad-based interest?

The company essentially changed how people manage the family photo album, making it digitally based. And all this started simply by the company offering online 4 x 6 prints and photo books. Last year, Shutterfly had a total revenue of 1.19 billion dollars. And all because Dan Baum, co-founder of the company, took a vacation. As an engineer at Silicon Graphics, while taking his regular vacation days, he tested photo image enhancement technology with a friend. Upon returning from that vacation, he quit his job and formed the start-up company with the simple premise of allowing people to print photos from an Internet site. The funny part is that Baum didn't really consider himself an entrepreneur! He just had an idea *so* self-perpetuating that the *idea itself* propelled him forward.

Now, obviously, whenever someone creates a landmark product or service like Shutterfly, it then seems clear that it was a great idea. And not all of you are going to create such an industry-altering service or product, but that doesn't mean you can't use the synergy you've already created in your team to elevate your process from achieving your vision to generating *more* vision. In the introductory chapter, I shared the story of what helped make me successful with the Harlem Globetrotters. The organization didn't just expect me to be a world-class athlete; they expected me to be a world-class athlete with my own style, my own strengths and my own creative flair. In other words, to make the organization great, the players brought to the court those qualities that made them tick personally. This was not only encouraged, but also expected.

So, how can you see your team not just as a means to make your vision a reality, but a means to elevate and even morph into completely unforeseen directions and results? You must *empower* them.

Yes, you have already empowered them to take your vision from theory to practice and from the drawing board to the showroom. But I'm talking about empowering them to add rocket boosters to your vision, to allow for some unpredictable and surprising ideas to be unwrapped. To utilize and *empower* your team to take this vision to a whole different level, you need to think in terms of two levels of empowerment: individual team members and your team as a whole.

Empowering Individual Team Members

The basic idea behind empowering individual team members is quite simply to free a team member to use his or her strengths more and to fight against his/her weaknesses less. Now, this will not be a new concept to anyone reading this book, because as an elite leader, you have heard this before. But *knowing* this leadership principle and actually *acting* on it are two different things. It takes courage, a little bit of risk, and a lot of patience to make this concept a reality with your team members.

By now, your vision is happening. Your team is functioning. The accountability you have provided your team has given feedback that improved your processes and performance. Now is the time to begin elevating your team members by analyzing and capitalizing on their strengths. I'm not talking about lower-level management decisions, such as whether an employee is better suited to work the register or flip the burgers. I'm talking about your core team of thinkers and doers, your top performers who have made your vision a reality. How can you make adjustments that will loosen the reins and let each team member run without constraint, still keeping the overall mission in mind? Let me give you four strategies to empower the individuals on your team.

Identify Their Gifts

Your team members have been so immersed in their particular roles in making your vision happen that they may not have had time for any introspection or self-analysis. But you have been watching the bigger picture. You have seen the duties and responsibilities that make certain members truly shine, seeing qualities they may not have seen for themselves.

After just a few games with the Globetrotters, my coach, the great Tex Harrison, pointed out the Showman at that time. A Harlem Globetrotter Showman is the leader, the face, and the voice of the team. Legendary Showmen such as Meadowlark Lemon, Sweet Lou Dunbar, Geese Ausby and Twiggy Sanders have delighted audiences for decades with their leadership, humor, style and skill. When Tex Harrison pointed out the current showman just games into my first year, he asked me, "Do you have what it takes to do this?"

I told the coach, "Sure, I can do it if you teach me." But deep down inside I had *no idea* if I had what it takes to be the Showman! That person carries the entire show and leads a team of well-paid experienced professional athletes.

In his funny, raspy voice, my coach responded, "Of course, I will teach you, son!" At that time, I wondered why the coach would have even asked me that question, but I found out years later. Coach Harrison said, "I could just see it in you, son. You were having fun out there; you had a lot of energy, and I saw your work ethic. I guess I was right." In fact, he was right. I improved so quickly under his mentoring that I got three pay raises my first year alone.

It is *your* job as the visionary team leader-as-coach to identify these strengths, talk to the team member about them, and even recognize them to the rest of the team. This demonstrates that you are proud to work alongside them, and that you have implicit trust in that person's abilities.

Revamp the Role as Necessary

To use the age-old illustration, instead of creating a round hole and trying to force a square peg team member into it, take a different angle. If your gut and experience tells you that freeing a team from tasks which are less productive and giving them more space for their strengths, let the team member assist you in creating the shape of the hole he fits in best. Average leaders hang onto written job descriptions as if they were holy and sacred; *elite* leaders write job descriptions around the people they have. Average leaders look to replace team members; *elite* leaders look to elevate team members by capitalizing on assets and potential.

Marcus Buckingham of the *Harvard Business Review* used a Gallup Organization survey of 80,000 managers followed up by a two-year close-range study of a few top personnel. He identified one quality that sets elite leaders apart from all the others: they discover what makes each of their team members unique and seek to benefit from those strengths. He calls this the difference between playing checkers and playing chess. He explains this dynamic as follows:

> In checkers, all the pieces are uniform and move in the same way; they are interchangeable. You need to plan and coordinate their movements, certainly, but they all move at the same pace, on parallel paths. In chess, each type of piece moves in a different way, and you can't play if you don't know how each piece moves. More importantly, you won't win if you don't think carefully about how you move the pieces... to integrate them into a coordinated plan of attack.[xi]

So, every once in a while, have your team members write a theoretical new job description in their areas of responsibility. You might be surprised at the increase in productivity that happens when you take this risk.

Learn and Grow with Team Member Eccentricities

Every team member will have their own particular quirks and peculiarities. These can range from little things such as wanting to have coffee at precisely 10:45AM each morning, to big things such as a deep need to verbally update you on progress every three days. For some leaders, these quirks can drive them crazy. But the elite leader will understand that these are the *keys* to the heart of your team members, which open the door to greater loyalty and productivity. Instead of getting irritated that your team member *must* have coffee at precisely 10:45AM each morning, give the gift of an amazing coffee station—or entire coffee *venue* if the size of your company allows it. Instead of getting exasperated by the constant interruptions of the three-day-report team member, be thankful that your input is so valued, and make time to be undistracted for those meetings.

Why is this so important? Because a team member who is valued for who she *is*, not who you *wish she would be*, is a team member who will put her best foot forward to make *you* successful. Here are three quick ways to grow with your team members' eccentricities:

- Have a team member quickly share an out-of-the-office passion with the team: biking, wine-tasting, family night at home, etc.
- Use a fun quiz tool to send out a quick Friday afternoon silly "mandatory" quiz. Pointless online quizzes have skyrocketed in popularity because they blow off steam and decrease stress. So, the occasional, "What Animal Would You Be" quiz with the results published in a later e-mail will bring a smile to everyone.
- Intentionally observe habits of your team. If one team member works better with a messy desk and another one is obsessed with total organization, adjust to that and let it be okay.

Identify Ways Your Team Members Can Help Each Other

While competition is what drives a great free-market economy overall, unhealthy competition within your own team can be deadly to your vision. They will have differing strengths and weaknesses and a focus on weaknesses can create a negative competitive and distasteful work environment. Instead, they need to be encouraged to look out for one another, to help each other. Now, make no mistake—*healthy* competition between teammates encourages productivity, fun, and strong working relationships. Using the team in order to solely benefit themselves (thinking only of personal promotion, raises, etc.) can create an environment of catty suspicion, but healthy competition in which teammates strive to outdo one another in excellence for the sake of the whole team is not only healthy, but also a team-bonding dynamic. But make no mistake: these competing team members have got each other's back when it counts. They are ultimately there for one another.

For example, you might have two team members, Benny and Jenny, who both must prepare data for analysis and present the results of this analysis to others in the company or to potential high-end customers. Benny is a little more comfortable in his world of being locked onto stats and figures and less comfortable actually presenting them to others. Jenny, on the other hand, is outgoing and can positively own a room with her personality, but isn't as excited about actually *preparing* her presentation. The average leader will send Benny to a public speaking seminar and chastise Jenny for her bad attitude about preparing her analysis. But the *elite* leader will team them up together to have Benny do *more* of the behind-the-scenes work and coach Jenny in what he has done, so that she can wow her listeners with a sparkling presentation.

Empowering Your Team as a Whole

Ask yourself this diagnostic question and be honest with yourself: *"Do I strive to succeed because of the emotional lift I get when others recognize me or because I truly desire to create a great product or service regardless of who gets the credit?"* The average leader must produce all the good ideas; the *elite* leader sees his team as an endless supply of *great* ideas. Your vision is a now reality; the wheels are turning; goals are being achieved. But how do you *empower* your team to surprise even you with their innovation? Let me give you five simple questions to ask your team to generate next-level progress with your vision.

"What if…"

When you were in the initial stages of creating your vision, this vision existed only in your own mind. You took this dream to your team who made it their own by adding their own unique qualities to the original. Now, instead of *you* necessarily being the one to yet again bring *your* upgraded vision to the team, you *empower* them by letting the whole team spark a new wave of ideas. So, you are not necessarily the one asking the team "what if" questions. Instead, you are triggering your team to ask *their* "what if" questions. Team members will have naturally analyzed their own role in your original vision simply by sheer repetition. Perhaps you are now 6–12 months into the successful execution of your vision. Now, each team member has expertise and has likely identified weaknesses or potential opportunities in their areas of responsibility. They must be given the freedom to ask:

- What if we eliminated this particular part altogether to streamline our process?
- What if we diverted just 10% more resources to this particularly lucrative part of our process?"
- What if I had an assistant to help me, which would triple my own productivity in this area?

These "what if" questions have the potential to open up new ways of thinking.

What are the top five things we are doing well as a team and how can we capitalize further on those successes?

The team will likely be able to recognize the most viable and exciting part of the mission they are accomplishing. As creative human beings, they will be able to give input to maximize what they are doing best. Now, I should say that you must have a trusting and positive team dynamic to ask this question. The team members who are working on *non-top-five* areas of importance can accidentally be made to feel inadequate. You as the elite leader must emphasize that when one team member succeeds everyone succeeds.

Sometimes when you are riding high on something that is already functioning well, you can relax and let the temptation to coast for a while make you forget to explore new avenues and new ideas. Analyzing what is already working and how to make it work *harder* for you is a great way to spark new innovations.

What are the less productive parts of this vision and how can we either streamline them or make them more productive?

This is obviously a sensitive question to ask because as I noted above, it can give the impression that a team member or parts of the team have failed (obviously, there may be those difficult times when a team member must be replaced or moved because of low productivity, but that should be rare). Instead, you remind the team that the whole vision is the focus. Certain parts of the vision will not function as well as others. In fact, you should free team members to be able to identify that *their* part of the vision is not contributing what it could to the overall goal. This doesn't mean those team members have failed; it means they have positively identified weaknesses in the system.

What are the ideas you've been itching to try?

Giving true ownership to every team member means that you have encouraged the creativity necessary to have experimental thoughts such as "I wonder what would happen if I did 'B' instead of 'A?'" But sometimes job security or an "if it ain't broke don't fix it" attitude can stifle risk-taking and innovation. The elite leader will not only encourage but also reward innovation with public recognition. If you have successfully created this environment, then your team should be freed to openly say, "Well, I've been dying to take a week away from my normal routine and explore this new way of doing what I usually do." If the team member makes a reasonable case, other team members will weigh in and perhaps instantly improve on that original idea. And you as the elite leader must have the courage to take that risk: "Okay, you've got it. Take that week and make something happen."

But let's take this question to a whole different level:

What are the ideas so crazy you've been afraid to say them aloud?

I came to America as child, but I lived in and was raised in Panama long enough to be proud of my status both as a Panamanian and an American. And one of the things I quickly learned that makes America unique is a long and storied history of a willingness to try crazy ideas. Some might even say that this is what made America great.

For example, in 1945, an engineer named Percy Spencer was working on radar sets at Raytheon using microwaves and discovered that the microwaves had melted the chocolate he happened to have in his pocket. To connect the dots from a technical engineering field to creating the device we now all use to pop popcorn, thaw meat, and reheat food—the common kitchen microwave oven—was nothing short of *crazy*—but it changed our kitchens forever.

In 1973, the United States Department of Defense developed the first global navigation satellite system to be able to help with navigation electronically by use of satellites orbiting the earth. What was once considered a crazy idea—that a piece of metal orbiting the earth could pinpoint my location *and* tell me how to get somewhere—is now the daily reality of GPS for all of us. Now we just talk to our phones and ask for directions. *That* is crazy, but someone had the guts to try it. Now, my phone can identify which applications I'm most likely to use by *which room of my house I'm in!*

So, your team must be given the chance to talk about the nuttiest, weirdest, most insane ideas ever. You never know when one of them will be the catalyst that changes *everything* in your vision and in your company. And by the way, if you have some particularly innovative people on your team, if you don't give them an outlet for that innovation, they will eventually find it elsewhere, and you'll see them in the news as they are marketing the product *you* wouldn't let them talk about. This need for an outlet for innovation was the impetus behind the original Google HR policy of allowing each employee to devote 20% of their time to their own projects. While the policy has been scrapped because of too much distraction from core responsibilities, the idea is a good one if practiced in moderation, and it has been followed by universities and nonprofits that grant sabbaticals to faculty and others.

The elite leader sees his or her team as the gateway to infinite ideas and advances. *Empower* them to let you plug into their skills and gifts for the greater good!

Chapter Six:
Smile

"We're so busy watching out for what's just ahead of us that we don't take time to enjoy where we are." - Bill Watterson

As a professional athlete and in my role as a leadership consultant, I have had many opportunities to interact with the media. I have been interviewed by everyone from *Good Morning America* to ESPN, *Fox Business* and even the *Cartoon Network*. But one TV personality who interviewed me when I was with the Harlem Globetrotters stands out to me as completely unique. He asked quality questions, but not because it was his job. He had a terrific smile, but not because of his professional demeanor. He had a clear interest in our conversation, but not because he was supposed to. And best of all, he was genuine and real, but not because of a seminar he went to about *appearing* genuine and real. He was as good an interviewer as any I had encountered—and he was probably 11 years old, interviewing me for a kids' sports television show.

I wondered why he was so authentic and so completely joyful about his job. I got the sense he was living his dream getting to interview professional athletes on a regular basis. But I also know he wasn't beset by adult worries such as making the mortgage payment, keeping TV ratings up, or some mid-life crisis. *He was simply doing something he loved and was having the time of his life!* How can you impart this climate to your team?

Your team members have the possibility of falling into one of two extremes when it comes to how work and business fits into life. On the one hand, a team member can clearly present as someone just living for the weekend… that work is nothing more than a paycheck. For this person, especially as a high-level team member with you, work has become an existence rather than a satisfying major part of life. Some people call this "burn-out." On the other hand, a team member can literally live and breathe career and success (this is more likely to be you as the team leader). This is sometimes called "work-a-holism." Both extremes ultimately drain the life out of the team member. The first extreme of the checked-out person obviously is an unhappy person who, for some reason, gave up at one point. The second person is constantly chasing emotionally addictive things, which ultimately do not provide real satisfaction, whether that's a bigger bonus, promotion, or prestige. Those things are nice, but they are also monsters that demand to be fed more.

So, how do you help your team members strike a balance… to be hard-working solid contributors who are thoroughly excited about your vision and the team's accomplishments, while still stopping to smell the roses at the same time? In other words, how can the collective team effort result in the final piece of my formula, *Smile*? How can team members *enjoy themselves* along the way, rather than just seeing their duties as either a tooth to be pulled or an emotional addiction to be maintained? How can you help them discover that they look forward to Friday as a reward for a job well done *and* look forward to Monday for the joyful challenges ahead of them? Because if you accomplish this balance you will have built a team that is a *success machine!*

Let me use one more acronym to organize my thoughts and give you something easy to recall. This is a memory help that reminds you to pause and make sure your team has a smile. If you want to bring that *Smile* to you and your team, you must remember to S.T.O.P.

S is for Smooth the Rough Places

Along the way in the implementation of your vision, parts of the project and even team members may go astray. You will deal with unforeseen surprises, attitude check moments, and even some frustration from team members at times. Your skill and instincts as a leader tell you that you *must* face those issues head on, including difficult times when you must give directives and correctives that don't make people happy. As an elite leader, you have already formed a vital relationship with your team members, so that these hard conversations have an underlying relational foundation. You have gone back to check in with that directed and/or corrected team member to make sure all is well and moving forward, and the issue is resolved. Thus, at some point it can be very helpful to revisit those moments from the standpoint of having worked through it already. Now, you are looking back with a little distance between you and that difficult time. This can be a quick conversation, but extremely meaningful to your team.

For example, Robin may be a team member who pushed back a little too forcefully at one point and threatened to derail the progress on her part of the project. You had to step in and provide an attitude check and be a little more direct and forceful than perhaps you even wanted to be. Robin responded well and got back on track. *Now,* you revisit this time with her: "Robin, a few weeks ago we got a little bit sideways over the such-and-such issue. I just wanted to come back and make sure you're okay and that we're okay. Is there anything I left undone or didn't help you with, or maybe even anything you needed to talk about?" Robin will either appreciate you for checking in and tell you she is fine, *or* she will appreciate you for checking in and give you a piece of her mind. Either way, you both win because that area of tension is resolved, and she can enjoy her work again.

T is for Tell the Story

What you and your team have done together *should not* just be allowed to fade away as last year's success. For millennia, human beings have relied on the verbal tradition of their tribes to pass on stories of great moments in history. And your "tribe"—your team—needs to have this verbal tradition as well. There needs to be a time you occasionally set aside to recount the saga of what got your group to this point. Maybe you are telling the story, or perhaps you are leading a group narration, including everything from key 'light bulb' moments to funny incidents (like TV and movie 'outtakes') not everyone knew about.

Story-telling reaches a part of the mind and heart that mere facts and strategy discussions can't even come close to doing. Business consultant Erica Sosna writes, "During periods of change and evolution, stories can be a powerful tool to help individuals within the business to adapt."[xii] Sosna reasons that human beings have always created comfort and security for themselves by tapping into the stories of their adventures, struggles, accomplishments and progress.

You may not think you are a natural storyteller, but I would assert that all elite leaders are *born* story-tellers; you just may not know it yet. You are a visionary, which means you tell a story in your mind… a story that begins as fiction and you make into reality. This is what you do *naturally*. It follows, then, that if you are able to tell a story about something you would like to see happen in the *future*, you can also tell the story of how it worked out in the real world.

Whether you take some time with your team to tell the story of how you all got this far, or lead a group narrative in which everyone pitches in, *tell the story*. It gives everyone time for introspection *and* creates a momentary emotional bond, which is a different dynamic than the business-as-usual meeting.

O is for Offer Your Gratitude

Any halfway decent leader knows the effectiveness of thanking your employees or team, but the *elite* leader knows a secret that average leaders do not know: *gratitude is more than just a leadership technique to manipulate your team to feel appreciated.* What do I mean by this? As a professional basketball player, I have played under captains of the team and many different coaches. And, I have walked in those shoes myself as the captain of the Harlem Globetrotters. And one of the duties of the captain is to express appreciation for effort and hard work. The thing is, *everyone* knows whether your expression of thanks is genuine or not. People are incredibly intuitive when it comes to sensing fakery in relationships. So, how do you as the elite leader crest the mountaintop to go beyond gratuitous go-through-the-motions thanks? Simple: it must be *real*.

What do you *think* about your team? Because, whatever you spend the most time *thinking* about will be the impression that eventually comes out in your relationship with them. You must cultivate thoughts of genuine gratitude about each team member. *And* you must catch yourself when you are defaulting to whiny negativity about someone in your own mind. Train yourself to think kindly and positively about each team member:

- "I appreciate how Howard doesn't push back when I change directions on him. He is always ready to adjust and almost takes it as a challenge."
- "I love how Dee puts that extra creative flair into everything she does. Her work is a canvas for her to paint on, and she uses every color."
- "Roger's accounting team is always on top of everything and able to help us adjust in real-time to current trends."

Ultimately, if you choose to continually focus on the negatives in your own mind, your team will sense your insincerity when you try to verbally express gratitude. But when you nurture the type of thoughts you want people to think about *you*, your genuine indebtedness and gratefulness will come through naturally. In fact, you will find yourself yearning to express that gratitude. It will no longer be a leadership technique; it will simply be a part of who you are as an elite leader.

P is for Punctuate Your Progress

While the idea of punctuation probably doesn't thrill you, unless you were an English major in college, we would miss it terribly if it wasn't present in both written language and spoken presentations. If for example I was to write about how you are to use my elite leadership formula but did not give you a place to see where one thought ended and the next one began and if there were no commas or periods or question marks then you would quickly feel confused and like you were on a never-ending terrible roller-coaster that you could not escape and then you would really really wish for just a period or comma somewhere somehow to stop the nightmarish assault by too many words…

See how much you hated that last "sentence?" Not only does language need punctuation, your *vision* needs punctuation. Your vision had a launching point and, just as importantly, you need a reflection point—a point at which you pause to consider what has happened. As you may have guessed, the first three parts of S.T.O.P. can all be geared around a punctuation point—a point to pause and consider. So, how do you punctuate your progress? Very simply, intentionally take time to reflect on what has happened so far, and in fact, all four elements of S.T.O.P. can happen in one punctuated event.

More than just having an ice cream Friday afternoon, or reserving a block of seats at a ballgame for your team, you need to punctuate your progress with some event that is meaningful, joyful, pleasant and reflective—an event in which you can *smooth the rough places, tell the story, offer your gratitude, and punctuate your progress.*

1 *plus one* = TEN

Putting S.T.O.P. into One Singular Event

For centuries, organizations of all kinds have recognized the value of a banquet or celebratory dinner. This banquet or dinner should have several major features:

- It should be a gift to your team to make them feel special;
- It should have great food (lousy food says they are not important);
- It should be in a fun venue away from the workplace;
- It should include spouses and significant others;
- It should include some fun (door prizes, giveaways, a short stand-up comedy show, etc.);
- It should—per your desire to impact the world—include something charitable, such as an opportunity to donate to the cause supported by your company; and,
- It should be your opportunity to address your team and do a S.T.O.P. speech or informal talk. It doesn't have to be long, but it should be meaningful and include all four elements.

Short Example of a Banquet Speech from the Team Leader to His Team

It's been great getting to spend some time together this evening at our Southern Neighbors Project Celebration Banquet. I've enjoyed getting reacquainted with some of your spouses. I hope you've gotten enough to eat—the dessert carts are still coming around!

[Smooth the rough places]—In the past months as we've embarked on what we decided to call our Southern Neighbors Project, as with any time you break new ground, there will be bumps and bruises along the way. I've learned a lot about you,

and you've probably learned more about me than I wanted you to know. When we had a major production and shipping crisis just a few months in, we had to make some tough decisions—decisions that didn't always make everyone feel good. But we worked through it, and you showed incredible integrity and determination to get us around that bump.

I put some of you into roles that were new and out of your comfort zone. I know that caused some angst and nervousness along the way. Some of you even expressed frustration to me that you were operating out of your element, but I believe I saw something in some of you that you had not yet seen yourself. And the fact that you are excelling in those roles now is proof that my faith in you was well placed.

[Tell the story]—It was exactly 15 months ago today that I was looking at some tourist information about Brazil for a possible family vacation. We had always wanted to go, and we thought this would be a good time to look into it. But then something hit me like a bolt of lightning. For a couple of minutes, I actually thought I was the dumbest person on the planet. Because, as I looked at a map of Brazil and began doing a little research into its demographics and other South American countries, I realized that I had been ignoring a massive new market that could literally elevate our business to be a world competitor.

I continued trying to plan this vacation to Brazil, but I would get up in the middle of the night and secretly look at websites about every country in South America. I wanted to know city populations, major industries, economic trends, and who else was selling similar products. I even tried to understand major social and political issues. I was so tangled in this that I finally had to not only plan our vacation—but I planned a top-secret trip to Brazil, Argentina, and Chile just to get my feet wet and try to wrap my mind around what taking our product to South America could look like.

Eventually, I honed my thoughts down to a simple two-page outline—still top secret because all of you would think I was nuts for what I was thinking. So, I came home—and I took Marcus out to lunch and, with trembling hands, I handed him my little plan and explained it to him. I still remember that he almost choked on his iced tea when I told him I wanted to double production within 36 months using South America as a brand new fertile sales ground. When he stared at me for the longest five seconds of my life, I knew he was going to do one of three things. He was going to:

- Laugh hysterically while he called 911 to have me committed;
- Resign on the spot on the grounds of working for a lunatic; or,
- He was going to say, "We can do this."

Well, he DID say, "We can do this." However, he added, "But, there are some major flaws to your plan." So, we hashed out a few things and decided to invite Sherry out the next week and pick her brain. When she choked, it was on mashed potatoes, not iced tea. But she did recover, and she saw some weaknesses that neither Marcus nor myself saw. But we hammered out a *reasonable starting point, and that's when we had the meeting with the top team leaders—I still remember you were all suspicious because we ordered a gourmet lunch to be brought in for the meeting.*

The long and short of it is that with the input of our top team leaders and the input that their teams gave them, we crafted a vision that the team named the Southern Neighbors Project. We had three simple goals: First, we wanted to double our own production and sales hopefully in 36 months. Second, we wanted to make a contribution to our industry in that the version of our product we have now marketed in South America is cheaper to make, 22% lighter, 24% stronger, and is unparalleled in these countries. Finally, we wanted to truly be neighbors to these countries, not just treating them as markets. So, the team identified one major charity that serves children in many of these countries and, with the help of our accounting team, we found a way to donate a generous percentage of all profits to these charities equally. In fact, many of you used vacation time this past year to go visit some of these charities and personally deliver our gift to them.

[Offer your gratitude] *I originally wanted to just improve our company's position in the world market and impact our bottom line, but I was surprised at the tremendous ripple effects the Southern Neighbors Project has had. I have gotten to know many of you and have seen the incredible gifts and talents that you bring to the table. I have seen determination and a belief in this project that has moved me to tears at times. I am thankful for each one of you, because without you, this idea would have died*

*1 plus one = * TEN

at my house when I was looking at a vacation to Brazil. You have taken a crazy thought and made it into a reality. I have written each of you a personal note so that I wouldn't drone on like an Oscar's speech—these notes are being brought to you right now and you will also find a little extra appreciation as well. And let me tell you why:

[Punctuate the Progress]—*It was our goal to double production and sales in 36 months, and at the 12-month mark in our three-year-vision, we are 17% ahead of our hoped-for pace. Because you believed in this project, 37% of you in this room are new employees this year with the new jobs we created to achieve this goal. Many of you have had to step into new higher-level responsibilities almost instantly and have knocked the ball out of the park. We tripled the size of our Research and Development department to roll out the new, improved version of our product just months into our quest. As of today, we have donated 1.9 million dollars to our charities in Brazil, Argentina, Chile and Venezuela. We just opened a new distribution center in Brazil and are months from a center in Argentina. And—remember that our second goal is to impact the industry—just several weeks ago we were approached by a Chinese company making a similar product, but without the R & D effort that we've put in. They believe they will not catch up, so they want to work together. I don't know what that will look like yet, but we have officially impacted our little corner of the marketplace.*

Tonight, I just wanted to pause—to stop and express my gratitude—and to congratulate all of you on an amazing feat. Monday morning, we hit the ground running again, but I wanted to lift my glass to you and tell you that it is you who make coming to work a joy and a privilege.

* * *

Do you see that this event (or an event with the same spirit of punctuation) is the result of the elite leader's vision and leadership? And, yet it creates a sense of satisfaction and joy because everyone took time to just stop and say, "Wow. Look what I'm part of."

You have the great privilege of being able to put a smile on the faces of your team… to see them thrive and have something to believe in. And, you did this! You did it with S.M.I.L.E.S.!

1 *plus one* = TEN

Cool Down:
Keep Smiling!

"The measure of who we are is what we do with what we have."

- Vince Lombardi

    1 + 1 = 10! If you will keep this formula at the forefront of your thinking, there is no limit to what you can achieve—and even better, there is no limit to the satisfaction you can attain for both yourself, your team and your company. Remember, to live a normal life of 1 + 1 = *2*—a life in which you work, earn a reasonable living, enjoy your family, and show up faithfully each Monday—this is honorable and a sensible way to live.

    But, if you have read this entire book, then I'm certain you don't *want* to be *sensible*; you don't *want* to be *reasonable*—you want to know that your efforts mean something and cause a chain reaction of good things to happen. You want 1 + 1 to equal 10, not just 2. You want to impact the lives of your team and the industry in which you operate.

    But remember the most important part of this equation, the first "1," is quite simply you. Do you want to order your life such that what you do has lasting implications, and so that no one around you, including your company, will never be the same? Now that you have come to the end of this book, will you do what I challenged you to do in the introduction? Will you take time to plan life changing and direction altering courses of action that will produce results *you no longer must personally make happen?*

If the answer is "yes," then now is the time for you to act on the second part of the equation, the second "1," the "IT" factor that I've broken down in my S.M.I.L.E.S. formula. Your goal is to create exponentially more *output* than *input*—to achieve the "10" with the input of yourself + S.M.I.L.E.S. Your life will be defined by moments in which you make decisions to do something different and step out into unknown territory—and take risks.

My Own Driving Passion

I am passionate about motivating people to do more than they thought they could do. If you read my award-winning autobiography, *I Never Stopped Smiling*, you know that in my own life it was adversity after tragedy, after pain that continued to drive me forward to succeed. I don't hold myself up as some sort of superhero; in fact, my point is just the opposite. I was just a normal kid who grew up in Panama amidst trying circumstances and made a decision to never stop pursuing my goals.

I still remember two opposite scenes that both have great meaning for me. I remember my older brothers and I not having a place to play basketball, so we nailed an old bicycle rim to our house for a "basket" and dribbled the ball in the grass. And, I equally remember the first time I actually got a paycheck for playing professional basketball. I remember the tears in my eyes, as I stared at that paycheck—because for me it wasn't money: it was victory. I endured the suicide of my mother, emigrating to the United States with my father, going to school in gang-hardened neighborhoods, clawing my way to a basketball scholarship, ultimately playing and studying at UCLA, and finally getting paid to do what I was made to do.

So, I just want to leave you with two important thoughts, the first and second "1" of the 1 + 1 = 10 formula.

You are "Number 1"

The phrase, "I am number 1," has an arrogant and brash sound to it, and usually when somebody says that, everyone around him thinks *less* of him. So, when I say, "You are 'Number 1,'" I don't mean that in the prideful sense. What I *do* mean is that the first part of the formula, the first "1," is *you and only you*. No one will aspire to greatness *for* you. No one will motivate you daily more than *you* will. When you set this book down, chances are you will have feelings of inspiration and motivation—but what happens *tomorrow* is entirely up to *you and only you*. So, let me suggest some questions for you to ask yourself each day, to remind yourself that you are the one who decides to aspire and to inspire:

- "Today, have I ordered my schedule for the greatest possible impact?"
- "Today, have I prioritized those things that are *most* impactful and put to the backburner those things that are the *least* impactful?"
- "Today, how will I inspire and serve my team?"
- "Today, how will I balance my life and inspire and serve my family?"
- "Today, what will I do that will create more *output* than *input*?"
- "Today, how am I working the S.M.I.L.E.S. formula?"
- "Today, what am I doing that will continue to have impact tomorrow?"

The Second "1"—Achieving a Lasting Smile

It is safe to say that perhaps one of the greatest marketing slogans in the history of commerce is Nike's "Just do it" slogan. In just three words,

Nike captures the essence of great coaching and of success in general. They give the dream to every person who buys their products that he or she has the ability to do more than they thought possible.

The second "1" in the 1 + 1 = 10 equation *is you making a decision to work the S.M.I.L.E.S. formula to the hilt!* You have looked in the mirror, made a decision that you *do* want to make the most of your opportunities, and now it's time to convince your team of the same thing—that *they too* can be greater than they thought possible.

Ultimately, the coach cannot get on the court or the field with you. And his parting words right before game time are the things he most needs you to hear, so here are *my* parting words to you as you get ready to step onto the court of your new adventure: You CAN do this!

You CAN brainstorm, and dream, and plan, and make something happen that will *astound you and everyone around you!* Do NOT just set this book down and say, "That was interesting." Start planning right now at this moment. Here is what you need to do *right now*:

- <u>Before you close this page</u>—get out your calendar and schedule time to review in detail the S.M.I.L.E.S. formula.
- Schedule a time and a place for your initial dreaming and brainstorming sessions. It might be on a beach in Maui, or at a local coffee shop. Just do it!
- Schedule a recurring appointment with yourself to review where you are on your journey to make 1 + 1 = 10 a reality. You *must* schedule follow-up times with yourself to maintain momentum. Remember, if you don't, no one will do it for you.

I can hardly wait for you to experience the first time you work the S.M.I.L.E.S. formula all the way, start to finish. You will never be the same. Your team will never be the same. Your company will never be the same. And the smiles you create will be life changing for you and everyone around you. Your team will now look to you with excitement and anticipation because they know that in *your* heart and mind exists some new crazy dream that says, "Let's keep smiling!"

Now Available on

Amazon.com

And

KevinDaleySpeaks.com

Notes

[i] Elizabeth The, "25 Fascinating Statistics about Employee Engagement," *Risepeople*, December 14, 2017, https://risepeople.com/blog/employee-engagement-statistics/.

[ii] Jennifer Costa, "The ROI of Employee Engagement: 7 Stats You Need to Know," *Business2Community.com*, June 21, 2016, https://www.business2community.com/strategy/roi-employee-engagement-7-stats-need-know-01573138#zYmqvmb8Hu5gSbRU.99.

[iii] Kurt Koffka, *Principles of Gestalt Psychology* (London, UK: Routledge and Kegan Paul Ltd, 1955, copywrite 1935), 176.

[iv] Fortune Editors, "Be the Boss, Not a Friend," *Fortune.com*, January 18, 2011, http://fortune.com/2011/01/18/be-the-boss-not-a-friend/.

[v] Jacquelyn Smith and Aine Cain, "28 Signs You're a Good Boss—Even if It Doesn't Feel Like It," *Business Insider*, October 18, 2016, http://www.businessinsider.com/more-signs-you-are-a-good-boss-2016-10.

[vi] Alison Green, "My Best Boss—Stories of the Greatest Bosses of All Time," June 5, 2014, https://www.quickbase.com/blog/my-best-boss-stories-of-the-greatest-bosses-of-all-time.

[vii] Fast Company Staff, "Announcing the Winners of the 2017 World Changing Ideas Awards," March 20, 2017, *Fastcompany.com*, https://www.fastcompany.com/3068873/announcing-the-winners-of-the-2017-world-changing-ideas-awards.

[viii] Margie Warrell, "Use it Or Lose It: The Science Behind Self-Confidence," *Forbes*, February 26, 2015, https://www.forbes.com/sites/margiewarrell/2015/02/26/build-self-confidence-5strategies/#79e9b15e6ade.

[ix] As told by Jared Brox, "Great Leaders are Great Delegators," *Refreshleadership.com*, February 23, 2013, http://www.refreshleadership.com/index.php/2013/02/great-leaders-great-delegators/.

[x] March 7, 2014 *Wall Street Journal*. Referenced at https://www.shutterfly.com/about/prs_sub_news.jsp#.

[xi] Marcus Buckingham, "What Great Managers Do," *Harvard Business Review*, March 2005.

[xii] Erica Sosna, "The Importance of Narrative," *BlessingWhite*, August 2014, http://blessingwhite.com/article/2014/08/19/the-importance-of-narrative/.

Made in the USA
Middletown, DE
31 January 2019